Everyday Life in
The Old Stone Age

FIG. 1.—Magdalenian Painting.

Everyday Life in
The Old Stone Age

Written and Illustrated by

Marjorie and C. H. B. Quennell
Authors of "Everyday Things in England"

G. P. Putnam's Sons
New York and London
The Knickerbocker Press
1922

TO

E. R. Q.

&

H. Q.

"The Masquerader"
by P. C. Q.

INTRODUCTION

THIS little book has come into being as a result of another that we wrote, and illustrated, between 1915 and 1919. It was intended for the younger readers, and we called it a *History of Everyday Things in England*. An attempt was made to draw the eyes of our readers away from the Destruction which was to the fore in those days, and to present instead a picture of all the care and trouble which had gone to the Construction of the everyday things that were being destroyed. We gave the matter very careful consideration, and it seemed to us essential that the things illustrated should be of a type with which our readers would be familiar. Some of my readers will have had an opportunity of seeing the Norman work at Norwich or Castle Rising, or the Renaissance work of Inigo Jones at Raynham. With some reluctance we made no mention of any earlier work. The doings of Roman, Saxon, and Dane were only hinted at,

Introduction

and the prehistoric period was not mentioned at all. We started with William the Conqueror, and finished at the end of the eighteenth century.

Since we appear to have interested many of the younger readers, we now want to fill in the long space before 1066. One is so apt to lump together all the earlier work, and think of it as having been done in a few centuries; the sense of perspective is lost. History is rather like travelling on the railway, the events flash past like telegraph posts, the nearer ones having their due spaces in between; but if we look back, the events, like the posts, are all bunched together and we cannot realize the spaces.

These spaces are as important as the events of History, and represent the periods when people were making up their minds; recovering perhaps from great disasters, or gathering their forces to go forward.

The races of mankind, like their works, develop by growth to flower and decay, but always there is a rebirth or renaissance. The Magdalenian Art we illustrate, died out in Azilian times, yet still lives to inspire us. If History is divided into events and spaces, then the people are divided into those who have ideas, and want to do and make

Introduction

things, and the others who only deal in the ideas, and benefit by these.

We hold that History is not just dates, but a long tale of man's life, labour, and achievements; and if this be so, we cannot afford to neglect the doings of prehistoric men, who, with flint for their material, made all the implements and weapons they needed for their everyday life.

Here is an illustration of what we mean. William of Malmesbury wrote in the twelfth century, of a monk of the monastery, Elmer by name, who made a flying machine and flew "for more than the distance of a furlong; but, agitated by the violence of the wind and the current of air, as well as by the consciousness of his rash attempt, he fell and broke his legs, and was lame ever after. He used to relate as the cause of his failure, his forgetting to provide himself a tail." Elmer was lamed because, being a pioneer, he lacked any history to go on; he did not leave any design behind him, but think how interesting it would have been had he done so. The twelfth century is hardly prehistoric, but sufficiently so to emphasize the principle, that there is something to be found out from work well done in any period.

Introduction

To describe the everyday life of prehistoric man is difficult, because there is not any history to go on. This is why we talk about these times as prehistoric. For any period after the Roman occupation we have the actual written word to depend upon; even before that, in 330 B.C., Pytheas of Marseilles sailed to Britain, and said the climate was foggy and damp, and the people raised quantities of corn. In the prehistoric period we have only the everyday things, and the physical characteristics of the earth itself; so the pick and shovel become more useful than the pen, and men dig for the information they need.

We call the pick and shovel historian an Archæologist, from the Greek *archaios*, ancient, and *logos*, discourse. The archæologist is helped by the astronomers and mathematicians, who are called in to decide in matter of climatic change like the Glacial Periods. A skull is found, like the one at Piltdown in Sussex, and the anatomists examine it carefully to fit it into its place as a link in the chain of man's development. The science of man and mankind is called Anthropology, from *anthropos*, a man, and *logos*, discourse. The science of life is Biology. Flint implements are found, are being found now by Mr. Reid Moir, *under* a bed which dates from Pliocene times. The geologists are called in, and the great problem is debated, whether man could have lived on the earth in this period. So one must know something of geology which is the science that deals with the structure of the earth.

A tremendous amount of work has been done in —what is from the historical point of view—a very short time. We give references in the text which show how very recent a growth is Archæology. If our readers are interested in this plan they can themselves raise a superstructure of more advanced knowledge, and to this end our authorities are named in this Introduction. We do not lay claim to any great store of archæological knowledge ourselves, and have approached our task rather as illustrators. As painter and architect, who have been making things ourselves all our lives, we may perhaps be able to treat of the work of prehistoric man in a sympathetic fashion, and hope our pictures will help our readers to *see* these old people a little.

This brings up the question of how we are to approach prehistoric man. We must free our minds

Introduction

of prejudice. Some people will say that he was a repulsive creature, incredibly dirty and unpleasant. Obviously this could not have been the case with the Magdalenians, whose work we see on p. 177. There will be other people who will regard our friend as the Noble Savage, and clothe him in their minds with all the simple virtues. It will not do to jump to conclusions. Shall we judge him by his WORK? If we try to find out how he lived, the tools he used, and the things that he made with them, then in the end we shall have a picture in our own minds. This is the essential part of reading a book, that it should help us to form our own conclusions. So we do not seek to teach, nor do we wish to preach, but we do want to interest our readers, and here we give you fair warning. If we can do so; if this subtle little microbe can work its way into your system, and you begin to grub about, and want to find out how things were made and done, then for the rest of your long lives the itching little worry will condemn you to go on grubbing, and you will become archæologists yourselves.

We should like to thank our Publishers for the trouble they have taken in publishing; Mr. Regi-

Introduction

nald Smith and Mr. O. G. S. Crawford for kindly
advice; Mr. Reid Moir for permission to include
our drawing of his theory of flint flaking; and our
very special thanks are due to Professor H. J.
Fleure and Dr. A. C. Haddon, who not only read
through our MS. and proofs with the greatest care,
but as well made many suggestions which we feel
have added to the value of the book. We are indebted to our friend Mr. Harold Falkner for information as to Farnham flints, and M. Forestier
and Mr. Cox, of the London Library, for
suggestions as to authorities.

MARJORIE and C. H. B. QUENNELL.

BERKHAMPSTED, HERTS,
September, 1921.

SHORT LIST OF AUTHORITIES

TITLE OF BOOK	AUTHOR	PUBLISHER
The Antiquity of Man in Europe	James Geikie	Oliver & Boyd, 1914
The Age of the Earth	W. J. Sollas	
The Antiquity of Man	Arthur Keith	Williams & Norgate, 1920
Ancient Britain	T. Rice Holmes	Clarendon Press, 1907
Ancient Hunters	W. J. Sollas	Macmillan, 1915
Man the Primeval Savage	Worthington G. Smith	Stanford, 1894
Man of the Old Stone Age	H. F. Osborn	Charles Scribner's Sons, 1918
La Caverne d'Altamira	Emile Cartailhac et l'abbé Henri Breuil	Imprimerie de Monaco, 1906
Pre-palæolithic Man	J. Reid Moir	Harrison, 1919
Rostro-carinate Flint Implements	E. Ray Lankester	*Proceedings of the Royal Society*, vol. xci.
Man and his Past.	O. G. S. Crawford	Oxford University Press, 1921
Science from an Easy Chair	E. Ray Lankester	Methuen, 1912
Guide to the Stone Age	British Museum	1911
Guide to Fossil Mammals and Birds	Natural History Museum.	1909
Guide to Elephants (Recent and Fossil)	Natural History Museum	1908

TITLE OF BOOK	AUTHOR	PUBLISHER
Guide to Fossil Remains of Man	Natural History Museum	1918
Manuel d'Archéologie	Déchelette	Librairie Alphonse Picard et fils
The Gravel Beds of Farnham	Henry Bury	*Proceedings of the Geologists' Association*, vol. xxiv. Part 4. 1913
Prehistory	M. C. Burkitt	Cambridge University Press, 1921
The Childhood of Art	H. G. Spearing	Kegan Paul, Trench, Trübner & Co., 1912
Naturalist's Voyage in H.M.S. Beagle	Charles Darwin	J. M. Dent & Sons
The Native Tribes of Central Australia	Spencer and Gillen	Macmillan, 1899
The Northern Tribes of Central Australia	Spencer and Gillen	Macmillan, 1904
The Aborigines of Victoria	R. Brough Smyth	Trübner & Co., 1878
The Aborigines of Tasmania	H. Ling Roth	F. King & Sons, 1899
The Central Eskimo	Dr. Frank Boas, in *6th Annual Report of the Bureau of Ethnology*, 1884–5	Washington Government Printing Office
Eskimo Life	Fridtjof Nansen	Longmans, Green & Co., 1893
Handbook to Ethnographical Collections	British Museum	1910

CONTENTS

Contents

ILLUSTRATIONS

Illustrations

Illustrations

Illustrations

EVERYDAY LIFE

IN

THE OLD STONE AGE

EVERYDAY LIFE IN THE OLD STONE AGE

CHAPTER I

THE A B C OF ARCHÆOLOGY

WE said in our Introduction that the archæologist is a pick and shovel historian. He investigates the lives of the ancient peoples, by the remains which they have left behind them; he needs must dig for his information, because the very earliest times are prehistoric, and no written word remains. To dig is to find out how the earth's crust is built up, and we must have some knowledge of its structure, if we are to understand the many evidences of life that we shall find. Geology, or the science of the earth, is of very recent growth. It was during the Renaissance, in the sixteenth century, that men first began to understand the meaning of fossils. In this, as in so many other things, Leonardo da Vinci, the great Italian painter (1452–1519) was a pioneer.

Everyday Life in the Old Stone Age

Here in England, it was largely due to William Smith, who was born, on the 23d of March, 1769, at Churchill, in Oxfordshire, that we now understand the way the stratified rocks of the earth are built up layer by layer. Steno, a Dane, who was a professor at Padua, had originated this idea, and published a book on the subject in 1669, but it was left to William Smith to work out the detail in this country. His father was a small farmer, and William had little schooling, yet by his observation of the countryside, by the time he was twenty-two he had constructed a system of geology; and remember there was no system before. When he was eighteen he had been apprenticed to a land surveyor, and later worked on the canals which were being cut through the countryside during the end of the eighteenth century. This work, of course, afforded him a splendid opportunity for observing the formation of the earth's crust. So, very largely as a result of Smith's work, we now know that the earth is built up of a series of sedimentary strata, and that these are in reality the sediment which has been deposited on the beds of old seas or lakes. These vary in thickness and position, in various parts of the world, but in all

4

parts they are in the same relative position one to the other. The earth is rather like an orange, with many skins of different colours, thicknesses, and materials; here and there a rude thumb has been inserted, and one or more skins torn out, but on each side of the gap, beyond the damage, we find the skins; rivers and seas may fill the gap, or the skins be distorted by blisters, or crinkled into mountains, but the principle of stratification remains.

Professor Sollas in his book, *The Age of the Earth*, has an interesting chapter on William Smith, and tells how he conceived the idea of representing the results of his work in a geological map. "Alone and single-handed he determined to accomplish in outline that which the organized efforts of H. M. Geological Survey, extended over half a century, have not yet completed in detail; and he succeeded in his task." William Smith has a further claim to our attention, because he discovered that not only were the fossils in the various strata the remains of living organisms, but that each stratum had its own peculiar fossils which were typical of the bed in which they were deposited, and the time when they were laid down, and that in all parts of the world they succeed each other in the same relative order. In classical times it had been thought that animal life could generate itself in the mud and slime of rivers and lakes, and fossils were regarded as specimens which had been left behind, or not properly developed, and so had been petrified into stone.

Geologists adopted and developed Smith's ideas, and by the discovery of the same kinds of fossils, in similar rocks in different parts of the world, began to be able to date them. In doing this they were attacked by their brother scientists who condemned this idea, pointing out that life must start at some definite point, and spread from this centre to other parts of the world. For the ordinary man, it seems sufficient to suppose that if you find the same kind of fossil in the limestones of America and England, and find the limestone itself in the same relative position to the other strata, then if the two are not twin brothers they must be most nearly related. The modern scientist can find out by observation how long the delta of a river, or any other form of sediment, takes to accumulate. In this way they form a scale by which they can also estimate the age of the older deposits.

To revert to our strata: The Chart opposite

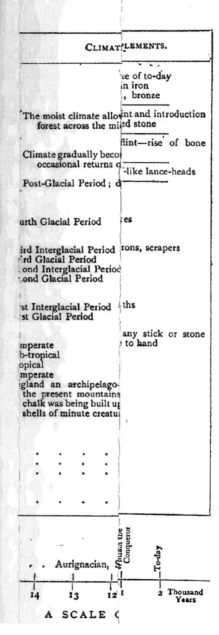

Climat	lements.

te of to-day
n iron
, bronze

The moist climate allo nt and introduction
forest across the mi d stone

flint—rise of bone

Climate gradually beco
occasional returns o
-like lance-heads

Post-Glacial Period ; d

urth Glacial Period es

ird Interglacial Period rons, scrapers
rd Glacial Period
ond Interglacial Period
ond Glacial Period

st Interglacial Period ths
st Glacial Period

any stick or stone
to hand

mperate
b-tropical
opical
mperate
gland an archipelago
the present mountains
chalk was being built u
shells of minute creatu

. . . .

. . . .

. . . .

Aurignacian, Conqueror To-day

14   13   12   2 Thousand
                          Years

A SCALE

GEOLOGICAL NAMES AND PERIODS				CIVILIZATIONS.	THE ROCKS.	CLIMATE.
Cainozoic (recent life)	Quaternary	Holocene (recent)		Steel / Iron / Bronze / Neolithic (New Stone Age)	Alluvial, Estuarine, and Marine deposits	The moist climate allows the spread of the forest across the middle of Europe
				Upper Palaeolithic (Upper Stone Age): Azilian / Magdalenian / Solutrean / Aurignacian (Reindeer, Shelter, and Cave Period)		Climate gradually becoming temperate with occasional returns of cold
		Pleistocene (most recent)		Mousterian	Peat, loess, gravels, brick-earth, boulder clay	Post-Glacial Period; dry cold winter
			Palaeolithic (Old Stone Age) / Lower Palaeolithic	Acheulean / Chellean (River Drift and Terrace Period)		Fourth Glacial Period
						Third Interglacial Period / Third Glacial Period / Second Interglacial Period / Second Glacial Period
				Strepyan		First Interglacial Period / First Glacial Period
	Tertiary	Pliocene (more recent) / Miocene (less recent) / Oligocene (little recent) / Eocene (dawn of recent) } 1600 feet		Eolithic (Dawn of Stone Age)	Norfolk Forest bed—Red Crags	Temperate / Sub-tropical / Tropical / Temperate
					Bagshot beds—London Clay	England an archipelago—the islands being the present mountains. In the seas the chalk was being built up from the calcareo shells of minute creatures
Mesozoic (middle life) ←Secondary	Cretaceous, 2,500 feet				Chalk—Greensand—Gault	
	Jurassic, 5,000 ,, / Triassic, 3,000 ,,				Portland Stone—Clays / White Lias, Penarth beds	
Palaeozoic (ancient life) ←Primary	Permian, 1,500 ,, / Carboniferous, 12,000 ,, / Devonian, 4,000 ,, / Silurian, 7,000 ,, / Ordovician, 15,000 ,, / Cambrian, 12,000 ,, / Pre-Cambrian (unknown)				Magnesian Limestone / Coal Measures—Millstone Grit / Old Red Sandstone / Downton and Ludlow Series / Bala and Caradoc ,, / Harlech and Hartshill ,, / Torridonian—Langmyndian	

The thickness of rocks as a guide to their age

(vertical) The Sahara becomes a desert — The Sahara a grass...

. . . Eolithic, Strepyan, and Chellean X . . . . Acheulean and Mousterian . . . . X . . . . . . Aurignacian, Solutrean, Magda

The A B C of Archaeology

shows the Geological Periods and the stratified rocks. These latter are shown in the order in which they were deposited, starting from the bottom upwards. To illustrate this more fully, we give a section across Wales and England (Fig. 3). We have Snowdon in the west at A. Its base at 1 is built on Pre-Cambrian, Cambrian, and Ordovician rocks, and there is an outcrop of these more to the east. Eruptive rocks appear at 3, and the Silurian at 4. The Devonian at 5, and at 6 the Gneiss at Malvern. All this west part of England has been disturbed, and the many skins or strata of the earth distorted by enormous physical disturbances. At B are the Malverns, and here there is a fault or break in the stratum, but as we go east the geological conditions become easier to understand; 8 and 9 are Red Marl or Triassic; 10 the Lias. At C we have the Cotswold Hills composed of the Oolites, 11; the Lias and Oolites are Jurassic. This is overlaid by the Greensand at 12, and the Chalk of the Chiltern Hills at 13; these are Cretaceous. Then we have the Eocene beds at 14.

We shall not be very concerned with the primary rocks in our study of prehistoric life, but shall soon come across references to those of the Mesozoic, or

Everyday Life in the Old Stone Age

Secondary Period. Here we find the Cretaceous, or chalk beds, and it was in these that primitive man in Britain dug for the flints he needed to make his implements.

Perhaps the next of our difficulties will be the constant reference which is made by the archæologists to the Ice Ages, and times when the climate of England was much colder than it is now; when we had glaciers here, and the North Sea was a solid mass of ice uniting Scandinavia with East Anglia. There are many theories as to how this came about.

We all know that the earth revolves round the sun on a path which is called its orbit. It completes the circle in a year, and turns on its own axis in so doing once a day, or 365 times in the year. As the earth turns round on its axis, the part which is toward the sun enjoys daylight, and in the part which is away, the people sleep because it is the night.

It is quite a good plan to make a rough working model of all this on the dining-room table, as Fig. 4, and if the family possesses a globe it will help. If not, let an orange take the place of the earth, and drive a knitting-needle through it for the axis. You can eat the Earth afterwards. A candle in the

FIG. 2.—Rostro-carinate or Eagle-beak Flint Implement.

FIG. 3.—Section across Wales and England.

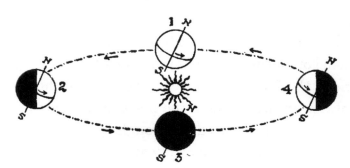

FIG. 4.—Causes of the Ice Ages.

middle of the table can be the sun. If the table is circular, the edge can be the earth's orbit; if not we can draw one in chalk. If on this path, the knitting-needle is placed in a vertical position, so that the equator of the orange, or earth, is level with the candle, or sun, then it can be seen that the equator will derive more light from the candle than the top and bottom where the knitting-needle comes through. So we discover in the case of the earth, that the equator is hotter than the polar caps, because it gets more sunshine. If we move the orange round the orbit, turning it as we go, but keeping the knitting-needle upright, we arrive at day and night, heat and cold, but not summer and winter, or why, when we have summer, Australia has winter; but let the knitting-needle lean over, and we have an entirely different state of affairs. This is what has happened, and to-day the angle of inclination of the equator to the orbit of the earth is 23° 27'. Our diagram (Fig. 4) shows how this affects the seasons.

The Vernal Equinox of 21st March is shown at position 1, when day and night are equal. At the Summer Solstice on 21st June, position 2, all the North Hemisphere will be turned towards the sun, and we get the longest days. At the Autumnal Equinox, 23d September, position 3, day and night are again equal. The Winter Solstice, position 4, comes on 21st December with the shortest day, and the Northern Hemisphere leans away from the sun and warmth.

The scientists tell us that this inclination of the equator to the earth's orbit, through long ages, varies from $22° 6'$ to $24° 50'$. The former would give us less difference between winter and summer than we have now, the latter would increase the difference. The shape of the earth's orbit changes, and sometimes is roughly elliptical, with the sun much nearer to one end than the other. This would mean short summers and long cold winters.

There is what is called the Precession of the Equinoxes; the earth wobbles as it spins, and this further affects the inclination of the axis. The Gulf Stream gives us now a better climate than our latitude entitles us to. When we bear in mind that the scientists tell us that a very small fall in the temperature would bring back the snow and ice, then it is easy to see how a combination of the conditions we have mentioned may have caused the Ice Ages.

The A B C of Archaeology

There is no need for alarm, and we need not rush off to buy skates in preparation for the next Ice Age. Thousands of years pass as the earth slowly wobbles on its journey. If we refer to the Chart, we shall see how all through Pliocene times weather conditions became colder, and culminated in the first Ice Age—then came a more genial time which the scientists call the First Interglacial Period, because they have arrived at the conclusion that there were four glacial periods, with three inter-glacial periods in between, and a post-glacial one after the fourth glacial period. We may be living in an interglacial period now.

The next of our difficulties may be the constant reference which the archæologist makes to the action of Glaciers; to large surfaces of land being denuded and deposited elsewhere, and to a period which is referred to as that of the River Drift. We will start with the Glaciers.

A glacier is a very slowly moving river of ice. Gathering its forces from the snowfields on the summits of the mountains, it moves by gravity down the valleys, and collects tributaries as it goes along. In doing this the snow solidifies into ice, and it is quite easy to see that a tremendous pressure must be exercised on the sides of the valleys. If we go into a mountainous region, which during the Ice Age had glaciers, we shall find plenty of evidence of their existence. The sides of the valleys have been worn smooth by the slowly moving mass of ice grinding into the rocks (*roches moutonnées*), there will also be piles of splintered rocks which are called moraines. The intense cold causes the rocks above the valley to crack and splinter, and fragments fall, and are left as embankments at the sides, or rolling on to the ice are carried along. These are called lateral moraines (1, Fig. 5). Where two glaciers join, these meet, and flowing down the middle of the lower glaciers are called medial moraines (2, Fig. 5). In this way glaciers transport materials for long distances. The débris of the lateral moraines falls into crevasses, or cracks in the ice, and appears lower down in the terminal moraines.

The glacier moving downhill, comes to a place where the temperature is warmer, and the ice melts. Here we find what is called a terminal moraine or moraine girdle (3, Fig. 5). These are generally fan-shaped, and represent the heap of broken rock and stone, which has been pushed forward under

14

FIG. 5.—Glaciers and Moraines.

the nose of the glacier, and gathered up by it in its progress from the bed and sides of the valleys. The existence of old moraine girdles, which have become covered with soil and trees, and now look like hills, is a proof of ice conditions in former times. There are girdle moraines as far west as Lyons in France, which prove that the Swiss glaciers were once of enormous length. High up on the sides of valleys, the *roches moutonnées* show that the glaciers were once very much deeper. All those facts help the scientists in their conclusions as to the duration of the Ice Ages, and the temperature general then.

Behind a moraine girdle, in the bed of the old glacier, we find a sort of enormous basin, filled with hummocks of boulder clay, called drumlins, at 4. To make this apparent the ice of the glacier has been broken away at 5. This clay is the mud which was brought down by the glacier, and was formed by the churning action of its underside on the rocks over which it passed.

Below the moraine girdle, we find what the Germans call *Schotter* fields. It is here, where the ice melts, that the river comes into being, carrying away the smaller pieces of rock, depositing them first in the *schotter*, then breaking and rolling the pieces until lower down we find them in the gravel formations of the river terraces. Our readers, perhaps, will know a river whose banks descend in terraced steps; it is a very usual formation. This connection between the glaciers, their girdle moraines, and river terraces is very important, because by their aid great men, like Professors Geikie and Penck, have worked out the theory of the Glacial Periods.

Professor Penck studied the river Steyr in Upper Austria, and found that each of its terraces connected up with the girdle moraine of an ancient glacier, and from this the following theory of the formation of terraces themselves has been evolved. Diagram Fig. 6 has been prepared to illustrate this.

We must bear in mind that before what we now call glacial times there had been other cold periods, and earlier river systems. Some great climatic changes must have been responsible for the extinction of great reptiles like the Dinosaurs, who, being large bodied and small brained, could not adapt themselves to change. The Ice Ages played their part in man's development; he learned to suit himself to new conditions and surroundings.

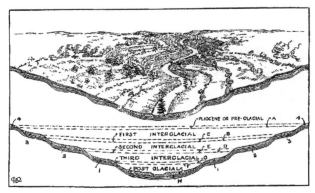

FIG. 6.—The Formation of River Terraces.

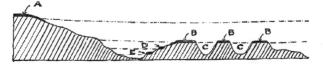

FIG. 7.—The Farnham Terraces.

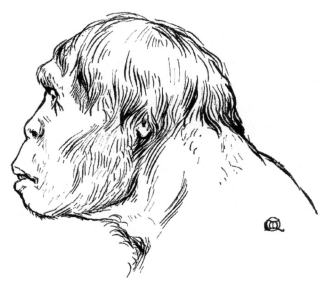

FIG. 8.—Pithecanthropus, the Sub-man of Java.

The A B C of Archaeology

Bed A in diagram Fig. 6 would be preglacial. In the First Glacial Period, at the end of Pliocene times, the volume of water in the rivers would not have been large, because so much was locked up in the ice of the glaciers.

Then came the warmer weather of the First Interglacial Period, when vast quantities of water were melted out of the glaciers, and hurrying down the old river bed, or forming another, cut a new channel to B. As the water lost its power to cut channels it began to build up the bed of gravel at C.

Then the Second Glacial Period came on, and the river again shrank in size. At the Second Interglacial Period the bed was cut down to D, and the bed of gravel at E built up gradually afterwards. The channel was cut down to F in Third Interglacial times, and bed G formed, and the final channel H cut in the warmer times after the Fourth Glacial Period, which we call post-glacial. An ingenious method has been applied to form an estimate of the time which has elapsed since the last Ice Age. As the glaciers retreated, during each summer mud was melted out of them and deposited in the form of clay; a band each year. In Sweden this is called banded clay, and in that country Baron de Geer has counted all the bands, and so formed an estimate of time.

To revert to the theory of how the terraces 1, 2, and 3 were formed, we have shown the gravels of which they are composed by a dotted surface, and it will be seen that they are in reality the edges of the old river-beds, which have been left behind as the water cut its way down. Our readers may think this sounds very ingenious, but demand some other proof, that all the terraces were not formed in one interglacial period.

This is supplied by the flint implements of varying design, and the fossil remains of animals of widely different periods, which have been found in the gravel formations of river terraces in many parts of the world. This is the period of the River Drift.

Our drawing (Fig. 6) can be taken as showing the terraces of the Somme at S. Acheul. The Somme is celebrated, because here it was, at Abbeville, that M. Boucher de Perthes discovered large quantities of flint implements in the gravel deposits, in the middle of the nineteenth century. As early as the end of the seventh century, a fine pear-shaped flint implement, which is now in the

British Museum, had been found near Gray's Inn Lane, London. Mr. John Frere discovered others at Hoxne, Suffolk, in 1797, and realized that those tools belonged "to a very remote period indeed, and to a people who had not the use of metals."

So that just as the fossils led the geologists to the theory of the stratification of the rocks and enabled the various layers to be dated, the flint implements and fossil remains of animals in the terraces suggested the idea that these had been formed at different times. The additional fact that the terraces of the Somme, Thames, and the Wey at Farnham, are much alike in general formation, and that in them are found flint implements which are of the same pattern, suggests that people of the same state of civilization once lived on their banks.

It will perhaps be as well for us now to run through the implements found in the terraces of the Somme, because it will familiarize our readers with the recognized French names for the various divisions of the Old Stone Age. We have no corresponding English names, so the French ones have been very generally adopted.

No implements have been found in the upper

Everyday Life in the Old Stone Age

plateau No. 4, which leads us to suppose that man did not live on the banks of the Somme before the First Glacial Period. In the next terrace downwards, No. 3, Strepyan implements are found. We shall explain what these are later; meanwhile, how did they get there? We have imagined a mighty river rushing down in flood at the beginning of the First Interglacial period, when the tremendous glaciers began to shrink and melt away, and this would be quite a different matter to the wastage only, which went on during glacial times. This flood of water is not an exaggeration. Remember that we are writing about periods which extended over, not hundreds, but thousands of years; as well that we are living in an interglacial period now. In September, 1920, a warm spell of a few days accompanied by rain after a rather cold summer, caused a serious situation at Chamonix in Switzerland. The papers said a glacier had "burst." What really happened was that the rise in temperature caused the Mont Anvers Glacier to melt more rapidly than its accustomed rate of wastage. Masses of ice broke away, and were swept with stone and mud into the valley. Rivers rose, trees were uprooted, and houses carried away. Now think of the whole of the north of Europe under an ice-cap, and the Swiss glaciers extending as far west as Lyons in France, and the temperature gradually becoming warmer. The scientists tell us that it only wants a fall of about 5° centigrade below the mean annual temperature of Europe to have all the rigour of the glacial periods back again, or that a rise of 4° to 5° would cause all the Swiss glaciers to disappear. So that one week rather warmer than usual in the First Interglacial period would have wrought tremendous damage. The new river-bed would have been torn out to level B, and the first layer of gravel formed by the grinding up of the rocks and flints deposited at C. Then perhaps the winter came on or dryer weather. The river shrank, and Strepyan man came down to the water's edge, he wanted to fish or drink; he may have camped there. In any case he left his tools behind and these were made of flint, and some are found to-day nearly as sharp and perfect as when he used them, neither rolled, nor abraded. The river rose again, and bringing down more gravel covered up the tools; sometimes it carried an implement along, and bruising it very considerably in so doing deposited it lower down the river.

Everyday Life in the Old Stone Age

In the second terrace (2) are found a few Strepyan tools in the underlying gravels. These may have washed down when the bed **E** was being formed in Second Interglacial times, because as the bed **C** over it was being undermined, the Strepyan implements in it may have slid down into the new gravels which were being formed under it. On these gravels sands were deposited, and in these early Chellean implements are found. So man again, during all the long years of the Second Interglacial period, lived on the water's edge of the Somme, and left his tools behind him to be covered up by the gravel deposited in flood times when he had to retreat up to the higher terraces. In the gravels of this terrace are found remains of *E. antiquus*, a southern type of elephant which preceded the mammoth. This shows us that the climate was warm.

In the gravels of the first terrace are found later Chellean implements, and the final gravel bed has not been explored because it is frequently submerged.

It should be noted that disturbances of the level of the earth's surface, in relation to the level of the sea, may have contributed to the formation of river terraces. For instance, well below the bed of the Thames is an old buried channel, in which the river ran, where the land was higher. Any raising of the land's surface would make the river run more rapidly on its way to the sea, and so have more power to cut its way down, and form terraces, or it may have been that the Ice Age locked up tremendous quantities of water, and thus lowered the sea-level. Since Neolithic times there has been little change in the earth's surface.

Fig. 7 shows the terraces of the River Wey at Farnham, Surrey, and we include this because it is nearer home than the Somme, also nearly all the flint implements illustrated in this book have been drawn from specimens found at Farnham. The gravel beds are shown by solid blacks. At A no implements have been found, so this may have been the bed of an enormous river of preglacial times which extended as the dotted line right across the country to Hindhead. The next river formation was on the line B, and of this there are gravel beds remaining on three ridges, valleys between having been cut since to C. D and E show rivers which were gradually shrinking to pigmy dimensions.

Everyday Life in the Old Stone Age

It is quite easy to see that such tremendous rivers could not have existed as part of our present river system. These old rivers were ambitious pushing fellows wanting more elbow-room, and this they had. The Thames at London stretched five miles wide between Highbury and Clapham. Europe in Pleistocene times had a different shape, and was a bigger place than it is now, and raised higher above the sea-level. The Atlantic was perhaps one hundred miles more to the west: the Mediterranean consisted of two inland seas.

The Irish Sea, English Channel, and North Sea were wide valleys feeding noble rivers. One, which we will call the River of the Men of Galley Hill, had for its tributaries the Thames, Rhine, and Elbe, and it discharged its waters into a northern sea just south of the Faroe Isles. Another, which we will call the River of the Men of S. Acheul, had for its tributaries the Seine, Somme, and all our southern rivers, and flowed westward to the Atlantic through the fertile *lands* of what is now the English Channel. England during some parts of the glacial periods was connected to Europe by a watershed of dry land where the Straits of Dover now are. There was an isthmus across

28

the Mediterranean at Gibraltar, and another south of Sicily. These trackways are very important because by them the Arctic animals could come south when it was cold here, and the southern animals come north when it was warm. This is the explanation of the hippopotamus in England: he did not need to swim, and was not cut out for flying; he walked here. In Aurignacian times the Sahara, till then a pleasant grassland, became a desert, and this led to the migration of men and animals.

Before we leave the question of rivers and their terraces, we must refer back to Fig. 6. On the upper drawing of the river the gravel of the terraces, which is shown dotted, is overlain by deposits which are shown by hatched lines.

These deposits are in the nature of Loess, or loam, brick-earth and soil washed down by rain, and have been a great puzzle to the geologists. At one time it was thought that great lakes were formed during the temperate periods between the Ice Ages, and that the deposits were made by the settling of the boulder clay which had been dissolved in the water; these would be called lacustrine. Some such cause must be looked for in the

Everyday Life in the Old Stone Age

thick deposit of brick earth at Caddington, to which we shall refer later, but this could not have been the case at S. Acheul on the Somme. Here, owing to the investigations of M. Commont, it is thought that these deposits on the terraces on the top of the gravel are what the scientists call sub-aerial, that is, deposited on the surface by the wind, as opposed to sub-aqueous, or under the action of water. The Loess, to which constant reference is made by the archæologists, is a greyish-brown sandy and chalky loam deposited by wind in the form of dust. This was caused by the action of frost during a glacial period. As the ice retreated the earth would have been a very barren place. There is evidence that at this period there were great winds and blizzards, which swept over these deserts and blew the dust about. This frequently led to the destruction of animal life, and their bones are found now in great quantities embedded in the Loess. The position of the Loess lands is very important; beginning at the Ural Mountains they stretch across South Russia to the Carpathians and the Danube, then by way of the north-west of Austria through South Germany into the north of France. The Loess did not lend itself to the development of thick forest, so this track remained open as a route for prehistoric man from east to west. Æolian is the term for a deposit laid down by winds; pluvial for that by rain. On the second terrace of the Somme at S. Acheul (p. 26) at its base, on the chalk, are found the gravels with the remains of *E. antiquus*, the southern elephant, and rough flint hand-axes, or bouchers, of Strepyan times. In the sands over the gravel are early Chellean implements, and these two layers were deposited by water. Then above this we start the sub-aerial deposits. First we have a white sandy loam with land shells. Above this is the older Loess, or Derm, in three layers, consisting of sands, and sandy loams, with gravel at base. Here are found remains of the red deer, and in the upper layer implements of the Upper Acheulean period. Above these three layers come three others of the younger Loess, or Ergeron, each layer divided by thin sections of gravel, in which are found Mousterian implements. Above this comes brick earth, which is weathered Loess, where are found Upper Aurignacian and Solutrean implements, and in the soil washed down on the extreme top there are implements from the Neolithic to the Iron Age.

Everyday Life in the Old Stone Age

(Refer to Chart and check the order of these industries.)

Think how bewildering it must have been to find all these evidences of ancient civilization in one and the same terrace, because not only were the implements found in the lowermost gravels of a later age as one went down from terrace 3, 2, and 1, but they also were later in each terrace as one approached the surface. It is owing to the genius of the French archæologists that we have found out all this.

In England we have had similar problems. At Caddington, Bedfordshire, Mr. Worthington G. Smith found an actual palæolithic flint worker's working-place, and how he did so is most interestingly told in *Man, The Primeval Savage*. This working-place was buried under brick-earth and clay, at a depth from 4 to 13 feet below the surface. Here Mr. Smith discovered flint implements of Acheulean type, with the anvils and hammer stones which had been used in their production, and specimens can be seen at the British Museum. These are sharp, and have not been rolled. In the 4 to 13 feet thickness of ground *over* these were discovered rougher implements of Chellean type which were earlier in date, and were covered with scratches or abraded, and had been rolled along. The suggestion is that man lived on the lower level, or palæolithic floor, on the banks of a lake, in one of the later interglacial periods, then an Ice Age came on, and he retreated to sunnier lands. At the beginning of the next interglacial period, a slowly moving, half-frozen mass descended from the higher ground near Caddington, and brought with it these older implements which had been left by earlier men still, and deposited these on the top of the later ones.

If you go to Caddington, you can see by the sections of ground which are visible in the brick-yards, how this contorted drift pushed along in a semi-fluid state and then came to rest. Truly, in the Ice Ages the old earth was cut and carved, shaped and modelled in a terrific way.

We may now sum up the problems which have confronted the archæologists in their studies. We started the chapter with William Smith's work on stratification, and this has enabled the scientist to gauge the age of sedimentary rocks by measuring the rate of deposit in modern formations. On p. 12 how the astronomers help by their calculations

Everyday Life in the Old Stone Age

of alterations of the inclination of the earth's axis; and on p. 18 how the girdle moraines of old glaciers and their connection with the river terraces give another clue.

Another method may be instanced. The scientist finds that there has been little, if any, difference between the appearance of men and women, or the domestic animals, of the time of ancient Egypt and our own day. This being the case, the Piltdown man (Fig. 10), *E. antiquus,* and the sabre-toothed tiger must be very remote, though it must be borne in mind that sudden changes of climate would have correspondingly rapid changes of men and animals.

Out of all these facts, the archæologists have endeavoured to form a scale of time by which to measure the age of these prehistoric civilizations, and this we have incorporated in our Chart. It should not be taken too much to heart, and need not disturb any boy's or girl's Faith; it seems to us a splendid picture; all these thousands of years, and man moving through them alert, resourceful, and plucky, and on an upward path!

CHAPTER II

THE STREPYAN, CHELLEAN, AND ACHEULEAN
MEN OF THE OLD STONE AGE

WE can now pass to a consideration of the most
interesting part of our study—Prehistoric man.
What did he do on the banks of the Somme, the
Thames, or the Wey; how did he fend for himself,
his wife, and children?   Or did he at first look after
himself, and preach the doctrine of self-help to the
family?   Perhaps before we endeavour to sum up
his doings, it will be well to take stock of his scanty
belongings.

Having done this latter, we shall then have to
look about for a model to help us.   A painter uses
a dummy which he calls a lay-figure; this he dresses
up and poses for the picture.   In the case of prehistoric man, our model must be drawn from the
savage races of modern times; and remember there
are still people who use stone, because they cannot
work iron, but such types are few and far between
now, and have lost their old self-reliance and in-

terest by contact with civilization. Obviously we cannot draw any useful comparisons between prehistoric and civilized man; they are poles apart so far as their lives are concerned; but, if we go back a little to the earlier voyagers, we can find records of people who were still living as simple and primitive a life as the prehistoric men.

Darwin started on his epoch-making voyage in the *Beagle* on the 27th December, 1831. He was not quite twenty-three, and was away for nearly five years, during which time he went round the world, and saw many native races. He wrote his book on *The Voyage of the Beagle* on his return, and if any boy or girl has not read it, it is a defect which can be speedily remedied, because there is a cheap edition in the "Everyman" series. We shall draw on Darwin, then, for comparisons. Even before his time the poor Tasmanians had been banished to an island, and had ceased to exist as a nation. They were an exceedingly primitive people, and fortunately for us Mr. H. Ling Roth's book on the *Aborigines of Tasmania* contains a most graphic and interesting account of all that went to make up their everyday life. Messrs. Spencer and Gillen's books have been drawn upon for details of the native Australians. Now for prehistoric man himself.

We have referred to the archæologist as a pick and shovel historian, because he digs for his knowledge. This means he digs for what is left of man. It is rather sad that man does not lend himself to the fossilization of his remains. He has always been a restless individual. The lower animals in kindly fashion seemed to arrange that their bodies might sink in the water, settle in the mud, and become beautiful fossils. This often came about as the result of drought—the poor beasts maddened by thirst would dash into the muddy bed of a river, and be too exhausted to pull themselves out. That they did so, has enabled us to find out about them. Man did not do this; he was too busy or too careful, and died out in the open; just dropped in his tracks, and did not think how inconvenient it would be for us—this neglect on his part to become a fossil. So his remains are very seldom found.

We have made a series of drawings of the types of skull which are known, and which are being referred to constantly by the archæologists, and which our readers are sure to meet if they begin to study seriously. Fig. 8 is of the *Pithecanthropus erectus*, or the first of the sub-men. In 1891 Prof. E. Dubois found the roof of a skull, two molar teeth, and a thigh-bone (femur) at Trinil in Java. The position is interesting because of its relation to Australia and Tasmania. The remains were found in river deposit of late Pliocene, or early Pleistocene, character. These were found in conjunction with the bones of many of the lower animals of the same period; but there were no implements.

The brain-pan of Pithecanthropus exceeds that of any ape, and equals about two-thirds that of modern man. Prof. G. Elliot Smith thinks that its features prove that the man belonged to the human family, and enjoyed rudimentary powers of speech. Darwin, writing of the Fuegians, said: "The language of those people, according to our notions, scarcely deserves to be called articulate. Captain Cook has compared it to a man clearing his throat, but certainly no European ever cleared his throat with so many hoarse, guttural, and clicking sounds." The thigh-bone of Pithecanthropus shows that he walked upright, but the teeth are more simian than human. Pithecanthropus was a link between gibbon and man. He probably re-

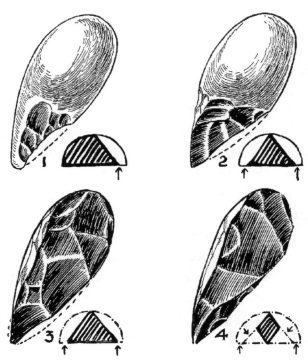

FIG. 9.—A Theory of Flint Flaking.

treated to the trees when he was alarmed, and may have contrived rough shelters or nests there, but of this, of course, we cannot be sure. The scientists went to Java because Europe was deserted by the man-like apes in early Pliocene times, as the temperature became colder. A more genial climate than ours was necessary for the development of this link, which, with brain, added to bone and muscle, was to connect them with us.

It is sad that Prof. Dubois could not find any tools or implements associated with Pithecanthropus, because it might have helped to clear up the knotty question of the Eoliths. These are very primitive flint implements (see **Fig. 9**), which one school of archæologists say must have been made by very primitive men; the opposing school contesting that they have been produced by natural causes.

Our readers will, we think, agree with us that the early flints (as **Fig. 18**), the human origin of which is unquestioned, could not have been produced at once. Thousands of years in all probability passed before early man got into his dull head the idea of shape. At first he must have used any stick, stone, or shell that came handy. Prob-

Everyday Life in the Old Stone Age

ably happy accident came to his aid; he broke a flint and found that it had a keen cutting edge. At the identical moment that it occurred to him to turn this flint into a rough tool by trimming it into shape, he took the first step towards civilizing himself.

When man discovered the use of fire, he had an ally which not only cooked his food and warmed his body, but would at the same time have sharpened and hardened a stick of wood, so that it could be used as a spear. Put any piece of wood in a fire and char the end; when scraped it is pointed in shape.

In *Pre-Palæolithic Man*, by **Mr. J. Reid Moir**, an interesting suggestion is put forward as to the development of the flint implement. We have made a drawing (Fig. 9) to illustrate this. Mr. Moir thinks that primitive man first used a split flint as 1. Its base would have had a sharp edge all round. Perhaps in use this edge got chipped, with the result that it became sharper. The flaking may then have been developed by man to make a scraper. In 2 this is done on both sides, with a resulting third edge or keel. By flaking all over the face 3 was obtained, and this is called the rostro-carinate type. 1, 2, and 3 all have flat bases. In 4 the

42

edges of the base have been knocked off, and a type is obtained which is like the Chellean implements we shall see later.

Fig. 2 gives a rostro-carinate or eagle's beak flint in more detail.

Our drawing of Pithecanthropus (Fig. 8) has been based on the plaster cast at the Natural History Museum at South Kensington. Here can be studied the fossil remains of man, and there is a fine collection of casts of primitive skulls. In drawing from these, it is evident that one may obtain an expression of character which may be either too brutal or too civilized, but the shape of the skull remains, and this determines the poise of the head, and many general characteristics of the face. We do not know if Pithecanthropus ever lived on the banks of the Somme, or Thames, because no human remains of his type have been found in England. His cousins may have existed nearer the equator in Africa, and their descendants then have found their way across the isthmus we referred to into Europe.

Our next illustration (Fig. 10) is of a very celebrated person, the Piltdown Man, *Eoanthropus Dawsoni*, or the Man of the Dawn, so named after his finder, Mr. Charles Dawson. We should be very proud of Eoanthropus, because he is the first known Englishman. In 1912 men were digging for gravel, and came across a skull which they broke up and threw away; a rather brutal thing to do, and in this case supremely foolish as well. One piece of the skull came into the possession of Mr. Dawson, who, recognizing its value, at once made search for the remaining portions. Other parts of the skull were found, a lower jaw, and later on a canine tooth. Since 1912 scientific men all over the world have written articles, indulged in friendly controversy, and found out all sorts of things about the Piltdown man. The remains were found in old river, or plateau, gravels, at Piltdown in the Sussex weald, the age and formation of which is uncertain, but in the gravels are fossil remains of animals dating from late Pliocene, and early Pleistocene, times, and as well the roughly worked flints called Eoliths; and some later ones, Palæoliths of an early type. Both the fossil remains of the late Pliocene and the Eoliths are much water-worn and rubbed, as if they had been rolled along, whereas the early Pleistocene fossils and the early Palæoliths have sharp edges and are not water-worn.

44

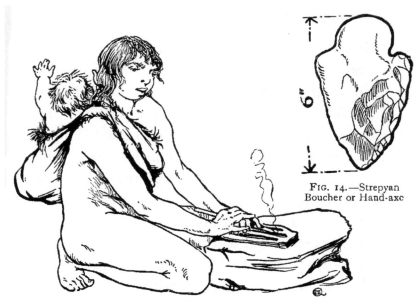

FIG. 14.—Strepyan
Boucher or Hand-axe

FIG. 13.—Making Fire.

FIG. 11.—The Pilt-
down Man's Bone
Implement.

FIG. 15.—*Machærodus*, the Sabre-toothed Tiger.

Strepyan, Chellean, Acheulean Men

From these facts the scientists assume that the Pliocene fossil remains and the Eoliths are older than the gravel, and were brought down by early rivers from some other land surface, as at Caddington (p. 26), and deposited with the stones which form the gravel. It is further assumed that the Piltdown man, and Pleistocene fossil remains, and the early Palæoliths may be of the same age, early Pleistocene. Boys and girls can judge this for themselves, because at the Natural History Museum at South Kensington, in the gallery of Fossil Mammals (Table Case 1), they can see a plaster cast of the skull, and the various fossil remains under it.

If this is so, then the Eoliths have to be accounted for, and must have been produced by some ancestor of the Piltdown man, who might have resembled the Java subman; though unfortunately no earlier human remains than the Piltdown man have been found in this country, and the Java man forgot to have his implements at hand when he started to become a fossil.

To revert to the skull, the Piltdown man is altogether a much more presentable person than his Java ancestor; he had a respectable forehead—a better one, indeed, than the Mousterian man of

Everyday Life in the Old Stone Age

Neanderthal type whom we shall meet later on. The brain capacity is about 1300 cubic centimetres, which is about equal to the smaller human brain of to-day; but with this evident increase in brain power, he still retained a very animal lower half to his face. The canine tooth is ape-like in shape, and would have been used as a weapon for offence or defence. The jaws stick out and give the face what is called a prognathous character. The skull is extraordinarily thick, 10 to 12 millimetres, as against 5 to 6 in modern man. The Piltdown man could, and probably did, butt a rival away, but notwithstanding all this he was on the upward grade.

The skull is what the scientists call mesaticephalic in shape, cephalic index about 78, and, as we shall be constantly meeting this and other terms used in relation to skulls, we will explain them now. The cephalic index is the ratio or percentage of the breadth of the head to the length, the latter being taken as one hundred.

Skulls with index of 70–75 = Dolichocephalic (long).
    "   "   "   " 75–80 = Mesaticephalic (intermediate).
    "   "   "   " 80–85 = Brachycephalic (round).

Strepyan, Chellean, Acheulean Men

For example, assuming a skull has a breadth of 135 millimetres and a length of 180, we get $\dfrac{135 \times 100}{180} =$ cephalic index of 75. If our readers have a large pair of calipers, they can measure up their friends, and inform them what their cephalic index happens to be.

One detail about the Piltdown man is, that the scientists think, by the shape of his brain, that he was right-handed. This makes him seem much more intimate.

As well as the Eoliths and Palæoliths, Mr. Dawson discovered a very extraordinary implement made of the thigh-bone of an elephant, and this cannot be later than early Pleistocene, because the bone of which it is made came from *Elephas meridionalis*, or *E. antiquus*, which lived in Europe in late Pliocene or early Pleistocene times. There were larger elephants than the Mammoth, who comes later, and had need to have been to provide thigh-bones of sufficient size to make this implement. It is 16 inches long, 4 inches wide, and 1 to 2 inches thick, shaped rather like the blade of a bat, and not water-worn; so, like the early Palæoliths, its age must be the same as the gravel in which

it was found. The use of the implement is unknown. There is a model of it at the Natural
History Museum, and we give a cut (Fig. 11)
which has been drawn from this. It will be noticed that the implement appears to have been
perforated at one end, so a thong may have been
attached here, and the implement thrown at small
game, and then retrieved from the thick under-
growth by being hauled back, but this seems a
clumsy way when stones were at hand.

Our next drawing (Fig. 12) looks rather like a
new design for the four of spades. This is not the
case; it shows the Piltdown man making flint implements. The ones illustrated are about 3½
inches long. The stone held in the right hand
acted as a hammer, and with this flakes were
knocked off, and shape given to the implement.
Flint flaking is an art, as can be easily tested by
trying to make an implement oneself. It is a
comparatively easy matter to strike off a flake,
but a very difficult one to shape it. The actual
idea of symmetry marks a great advance, and is
the beginning of a sense of proportion; a feeling
that the implement will not only cut as well as the
rough flake, but that it would look better, and be

FIG. 12.—Piltdown Man making Flint Implement.

more pleasant to handle, if it were shaped. It is this shaping which makes us feel that the Eoliths must have been made by humans, because we cannot believe that they would arrive at the stage shown in Fig. 12 without endless experiment.

These flints of the Piltdown man are presentable-looking objects; he has begun to take a pride in his work, which, when you come to think about it, is the most satisfactory emotion that boy or man can experience.

These implements would have had all sorts of uses. Flint can be made as sharp as a razor, and they served as the knives of the day, and were used to cut up a beast, scrape a bone, dig up pig-nuts or shape a stick. Flint is extraordinarily hard—until quite recently it was used in connection with steel and tinder to produce fire. If a piece is struck against steel, minute fragments of the latter fly off, heated by the blow to such an extent that they burn in the air as sparks. Prehistoric man probably obtained his fire in this way, using, instead of steel, marcasite, an iron sulphide found in association with flint, or he may have done so by friction, rubbing one piece of wood up and down in a groove in another piece, until the dust ignited (see Fig. 13).

Everyday Life in the Old Stone Age

We will now refer back to our diagram (Fig. 6), and go into the detail of the implements which are found on the banks of the Somme. In the gravels of terrace No. 3, the worked flints are said to be of Strepyan, or pre-Chellean, design. Strépy is a place in Belgium. The implements are roughly flaked, and generally have some part of the original crust remaining. Fig. 14 shows a rough form of boucher, a term invented by Prof. Sollas, in honour of M. Boucher de Perthes, who first found worked flints on the Somme. The French call this a *coup de poing;* hand-axe is another term. The boucher was held in the hand, but, we think, not as a dagger, point down; we say this, because in the collection of our friend, Harold Falkner of Farnham, all the points are intact, and only the side edges show signs of wear. We think the butt was held in the palm of the hand, with the first finger along one edge, to cut with the other.

Strepyan man also used flints fashioned for scraping fat off the skins of the animals he killed, and the bark off all the odd pieces of wood that he must have needed. His spears would have been of wood. When he lived on the banks of the Somme in the First Interglacial period, he had as com-

FIG. 16.—The Pitfall.

FIG. 17.—Galley Hill Man.

panions two huge elephants, E. *meridionalis* and *E. antiquus;* the hippopotamus, rhinoceros, and sabre-toothed tiger; and a horse, *E. stenonis.* The naturalists tell us that the teeth of *E. antiquus* were adapted to eating the small branches and foliage of trees. This gives an interesting indication of the Strepyan climate. It must have been warm and genial for these southern animals to have flourished.

How man fended for himself we cannot tell; armed only with a boucher, which he perhaps hafted as a spear, he could have but little chance against an elephant, 15 feet high to the top of the shoulder.

If looks are any criterion, the sabre-toothed tiger, *Machærodus* (Fig. 15), must have been an evil beast. There is a plaster cast of one at the Natural History Museum. Machærodus was widely distributed and existed in England with the cave men who came later on; this we know because his teeth have been found in Kent's Cavern and Cresswell Caves. Man could only have combated such animals by craft; fire and traps were his weapons, and one expects that he was not too proud to eat the remains of the tiger's feast. Fig. 16 is of a pitfall in use by the natives of British East Africa. Labour was plentiful in Strepyan days, and everybody lent a hand. To dig the pit would not have been beyond the wit of prehistoric man, and the stakes could have been sharpened and the points hardened by fire. Such a pit would have been a beginning of the long battle between brain and mere bulk. This would have been one way in which prehistoric man obtained the meat that he needed for his food. He was, of course, as carnivorous as his foe the tiger. He possessed neither flocks, nor herds, and did not grow any corn.

Darwin tells us that "the Gaucho in the Pampas, for months together, touches nothing but beef. But they eat, I observe, a very large proportion of fat."

Again, Darwin gives us a splendid picture of how to support life, when there is not a butcher's shop just round the corner, but you have to catch your supper before you can cook it. He was in the Falkland Islands at the time. His Gaucho separated a fat cow from a herd of wild cattle, and caught it with his *lazo*. It was then hamstrung, and killed by driving a knife "into the head of the spinal marrow." These details are given because, when you are a prehistoric man, you can't afford to be sensitive. A large circular piece of flesh was then cut out of the back, with the skin

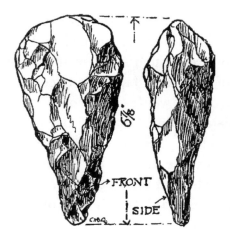

FRONT

SIDE

FIG. 18.—Chellean Boucher or
Hand-axe.

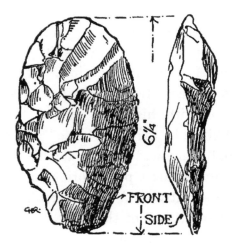

FRONT

SIDE

FIG. 19.—Oval Implement.

attached; this was roasted on the embers, with the hide downwards and in the form of a saucer, so that none of the gravy was lost.

Though the weather was wet, the Gauchos managed to light their fire. First with their flint and steel they get a spark on to their piece of charred rag or tinder. Then "they sought beneath the tufts of grass and bushes for a few dry twigs, and these they rubbed into fibres; then surrounding them with coarser twigs, something like a bird's nest, they put the rag with its spark of fire in the middle and covered it up. The nest being then held up to the wind, by degrees it smoked more and more, and at last burst out in flames."

For fuel the Gauchos "found what, to my surprise, made nearly as hot a fire as coals, this was the skeleton of a bullock lately killed, from which the flesh had been picked by the carrion hawks."

Darwin enjoyed his supper, and recommended "*carne con cuero.*"

CHELLEAN MAN

The next stage in man's development, which is recognized by the archæologists, is that called

Everyday Life in the Old Stone Age

"Chellean." This name comes from Chelles, on the Seine, near Paris. There has been considerable controversy as to what Chellean man was like. Here in England at Galley Hill, Swanscombe, Kent, a skeleton was found in 1888, which we illustrate (Fig. 17), and which Sir Arthur Keith contends is that of a Chellean man. The head is of great length, but not very high. The skull is very thick, the eyebrow ridges not nearly so much developed as in the later Neanderthal type. The chin is beginning to be quite modern, but the teeth are primitive. It may well be that here in England in Chellean times the men were developed who in the end became *homo sapiens*. Chellean implements are found in Swanscombe which correspond to those found in the sands above the lower gravels of the second terrace of the Somme (Fig. 6). Later types are found in the first terrace.

The boucher (Fig. 18) has developed since Strepyan times. It was still formed by knocking flakes off a flint nodule, and remains the most useful tool of prehistoric man; but the Chellean boucher is quite a well-made implement, and the man who made it was becoming a good craftsman. His flint work was far in advance of that of the

FIG. 20.—Chellean Scraper.

FIG. 22.—A Break-wind.

FIG. 21.—Falling Spear.

Tasmanians. Sometimes it has a thick butt end, and a longer point, while others are oval in shape as Fig. 19. The earlier the type, the thicker the implement. Fig. 20 shows a woman using a flint scraper, one of the most useful implements of prehistoric man.

The people who know how to make these flints were widely distributed. Prof. Sollas says that bouchers are found in all the continents of the world, except Australia.

Many hundreds of flint implements are often found in the same gravel pit, and this is thought to prove that large numbers of prehistoric people camped together. This is doubtful; food was scarce. It is, of course, always difficult to remember that an interglacial period extended over thousands of years, so that if a river bank was a favourite camping-place, the tools could have been dropped year after year, and covered up by gravel and sand in times of flood. We dig these to-day, and forget the long time which it took for the gravel to be deposited. Another point to be borne in mind is that, so far, all the remains of prehistoric man that we have noted have been found near water. The men of the river drift had to camp by the side of a river, or lake, because they had not any pots or pans in which to store water. Thousands of years passed before man made pottery.

Another point to remember is, the one which was pointed out to the nineteenth-century geologists in regard to the same sort of fossils found in the rocks in different parts of the world: these were not all living organisms at the same time. Life proceeds from a centre and spreads. So this widely distributed Chellean civilization did not start all over the world at one given minute. If it started in India, or Africa, it took time for it to reach the Wey, by the isthmus across the Straits of Dover. Prehistoric man was a great traveller, and that by the most urgent necessity of all: the need to find food. Darwin mentions two Spanish girls taken captive by Indians. "From their account they must have come from Salta, a distance in a straight line of nearly one thousand miles. This gives one a grand idea of the immense territory over which the Indians roam." So it was with prehistoric man. Remember he started as a hunter, then developed into a herdsman, then became a farmer, and settled down to guard his possessions. Remember as well that we call the industry Chellean,

Strepyan, Chellean, Acheulean Men

not because it originated at Chelles, but by reason of the wonderful way the French archæologists have explored the remains of prehistoric man; they have done this so well that we have adopted their names for want of better ones of our own.   England must have been an outpost of Chellean civilization.

Chellean man had to encounter much the same sort of animals as those of Strepyan times.   The huge *Elephas antiquus* remained as a problem for the hunters to tackle.   They probably employed the pitfall to trap animals; the Australians still catch emus in this way, or they may have been the inventors of another device which is still employed by native races.   This consists of a large and heavy piece of wood, which is suspended above a path, pointing downwards, by a grass rope.   Fig. 21 shows how the animal, pushing its way along, cracks the rope, with the result that the spear falls on to the spinal column.

We may turn to Darwin to gain information as to the appearance of savage races.   Writing of the Fuegians he said: "Their only garment consists of a mantle made of quanaco skin, with the wool outside; this they wear just thrown over their shoulders."   But the skin cloak appears to have been a party frock, and not for general use. Darwin saw them in their canoes; the sleet falling, and thawing on their naked bodies. He refers to the Fuegian wigwam which "resembles, in size and dimensions, a hay-cock. It merely consists of a few broken branches stuck in the ground, and very imperfectly thatched on one side with a few tufts of grass and rushes. . . . At Goeree Roads I saw a place where one of these naked men had slept, which absolutely offered no more cover than the form of a hare."

The Tasmanians made much the same form of shelter, using bark instead of grass and rushes, and we have shown the type in Fig. 22. Treat the drawing with respect, because it shows house No. 1. They also went about quite naked, using occasionally a fur cloak. Both the Fuegians and the Tasmanians liberally anointed their bodies and heads with grease mixed with the ochreous earths. In this way they gained a certain protection from the weather, and it helped to keep them clean. Earth is a fine deodorizer. There is a good tale told of a party of Tasmanians given some soup, on the top of which floated fat; this they scooped off with their hands, and put on their heads, but they did not drink the soup. Primitive man almost invariably roasts or bakes his meat.

Later on we give instances of human remains being found, buried with red ochre, for use in the spirit world. This points to the covering of grease and ochre, having developed from a protection into a decoration of the body.

Darwin wrote of the Fuegians: "The old man had a fillet of white feathers tied round his head, which partly confined his black, coarse, and entangled hair. His face was crossed by two broad transverse bars; one painted bright red, reached from ear to ear and included the upper lip; the other, white like chalk, extended above and parallel to the first, so that even his eyelids were thus coloured."

We have just referred to skeletons being found with colour for decorating the body, and implements for use in the spirit world, and such burials point to a belief in a future life. But we can find no traces as yet of such a belief on the part of the Chellean man. Captain FitzRoy of the *Beagle* could never ascertain that the Fuegians had any distinct belief in a future life. When driven by extreme hunger they killed and ate the old women, before their dogs, because, as they said, "Doggies catch otters, old women no." In the Uganda, before a human sacrifice, the victim was made to drink from a magic cup to destroy his soul first. A horrible idea, but yet proving that even the most degraded types as a rule believe in a future life.

As to what the Chelleans believed, we cannot say.

Acheulean Man

We can now turn to Acheulean types of implements. Here we still have the boucher (Fig. 23), but it is a much better one; thinner and more finely flaked, with a truer edge. Scrapers were used as well, but Acheulean man does not seem to have had many more sorts of implements than his Chellean ancestor. It must be borne in mind that these names are terms used to denote certain stages in the development of flint implements. In reality the design of these was a continued growth, and prehistoric man did not, in any one year, leave off making Chellean types and introduce a new Acheulean fashion.

In the description of the sub-aerial deposits on the terraces of the Somme (p. 31), we noted that

G. 23.—An Acheulean Boucher
or Hand-axe.

FIG. 24.—*Elephas primigenius*, the Mammoth.

FIG. 25.—*Rhinoceros tichorhinus*, the Woolly-coated Rhinoceros.

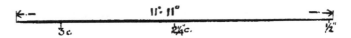

FIG. 26.—Tasmanian Spear.

Strepyan, Chellean, Acheulean Men

the earliest Acheulean types are found in the sands and gravels at the base of the lower Derm, and the later types in the lowest strata of the older Loess. This older Loess is in three layers, and in the middle and upper layers no implements are found. It is supposed to have been deposited in glacial times so it seems as if the weather gradually became too cold for man to camp by the riverside. This view is borne out by the remains of the animals found and in the implements. In the sand and gravel of the earlier Acheulean times, we have our old friend *E. antiquus* and the red deer, both southern animals; but in the later Acheulean of the lowest layer of the older Loess, we meet for the first time, *E. primigenius* (the mammoth), *Rhinoceros tichorhinus* (the woolly-coated one), horse, and lion. These were northern animals who came south as the weather became colder and the Fourth Glacial period drew on.

The mammoth was not so large as *E. antiquus*, and closely resembled the existing Indian elephant, excepting only the tusks, which are very long and curved. Its teeth were more adapted for eating coarse grasses than the foliage of trees. The country was becoming barer and bleaker, and trees were scarce. Its curved tusks perhaps acted as hay-rakes, and helped to gather up food. Its warm coat and thick skin, with a layer of fat under, pro-tected it from the cold weather. We know all about the mammoth, because whole carcases have been dug up in the frozen Arctic regions, with the flesh, skin, and furry coats, protected through the ages by the ice and snow in which they were em-bedded. Our sketch (Fig. 24) gives a general idea of this animal, and Fig. 25 shows the woolly-coated rhinoceros.

If reference is made to the Chart, it will be seen that during Acheulean times the weather was get-ting colder, and as the ice-cap crept down, so these animals from the northern regions retreated before it. Man appears for the same reason to have looked about for warmer shelter than the open-air camps, and to have retreated to the caves and caverns.

Before we pass on to the Cave-dwellers, let us sum up what we have found out about prehistoric man, and draw some comparisons. We say that he was a nomad and a hunter, but unless we are careful to think a little, the mental picture we form is of some one rather like ourselves; a little rougher perhaps, and more whiskery, but with a background of solid comfort somewhere. We shall be right in imagining the Chellean a man like ourselves, with an active brain, but comfort as we understand it did not exist for him.

We do not realize that prehistoric man was a nomad, or wanderer, because he had to hunt for his food; that unless he hunted he starved. It is really extremely difficult to imagine a state of affairs when a man's sole possessions consisted of a flint boucher for tool; a wooden spear for a weapon, and a skin for covering; when all else had to be searched for; when pots and pans did not exist; when pottery and weaving had not been invented. Yet such people have existed until comparatively recent times. Tasmania was discovered in 1642, by Abel Janszoon Tasman, who named it Van Diemen's Land, after Anthony Van Diemen, the Governor of the Dutch East Indies. In an amusing way it has been renamed after its discoverer. After his time Tasmania was visited by other voyagers, Captain Cook being one in 1777, and they found the Tasmanians to be to all intents and purposes a prehistoric people. It seems as if, in remote ages, when Asia, like Europe, had a different coastline, the Tasmanians had come from the mainline into Australia and, retreating again before stronger races, found their way in the end into Tasmania, before it was so much cut off as it is now. There may have been an isthmus across Bass Strait, as there was in Europe across the Straits of Dover. At some later period this disappeared, and the Tasmanians were left free to remain the simple primitive folk they were when first discovered.

They had not the use of iron, and their only tools were made of flint, and very rough ones at that. They had not any "boucher" which was as good a piece of work as that of Chellean man (Fig. 19). Generally the Tasmanians went about quite naked, but on occasions wore a skin cloak. Kangaroo skins were dressed as rugs to sit upon. Wet and cold did not appear to harm them, and their houses, as Fig. 22, were the merest break-winds. When in 1831 the miserable remainder of the natives were exiled to Flinders Island, and lodged in huts, it was found that they caught cold far more readily than when living in the open. Like the Fuegians in their native state, they greased their bodies, and anointed themselves with red ochre; this gave a certain protection.   They were also fond of making necklaces of shells, and ornamented their bodies by forming patterns of scars (cicatrization) left by cuts made with a sharp flint.   They were nomads moving about the country in search of food; this meant that in hard times the very old and infirm people were left to die, and sometimes the babies had to be sacrificed.

In hunting game like kangaroo they used plain spears, as Fig. 26, made of a hard wood.   This is not quite the simple thing it seems.   Pithecan-thropus would have picked up any long stick to hit with, and it may have slipped from his hand.   He then discovered that unless one end was heavier than the other, it did not follow a very straight line of flight; it might knock down a bird, but would not pierce with its point the skin of an animal, so through the long ages the Tasmanian spear de-veloped.   This was cut, trimmed, and scraped with flint.   Straightened by being passed over a fire, the teeth were used instead of the later shaft-straightener (Fig. 46).   The end was charred by fire, and so hardened, and then pointed by scrap-ing.   The point was at the heavy end; 20 inches from this the circumference was 3 inches, in the

Everyday Life in the Old Stone Age

middle 2¼ inches, and 2 inches from the end only ½ inch. The total length was 11 feet 11 inches. The Tasmanian could throw this, and kill an animal at from 40 to 50 yards, and did not use a throwing-stick, as Fig. 34. Unlike the Australians, they used neither boomerangs nor shields. Their other weapon was the waddy, or wooden club, about 2 feet 6 inches long, and they threw stones with great accuracy.

The Tasmanian wooden spear had its counterpart in England in the Old Stone Age. In a very interesting book just published, written by Mr. O. G. S. Crawford, and called *Man and his Past*, is an illustration of what is probably the only known palæolithic wooden object. It is apparently the broken head of a wooden spear about 15 inches long, pointed at one end, and about 1½ inches diameter at the other. It looks exactly as if the end had been broken off the Tasmanian spear (Fig. 26), and was found at Clacton in Essex, in the *E. antiquus* bed in association with an early type of flint implement.

It may well be, that here in England, Chellean man hunted and killed smaller game than this southern elephant; to have attacked *E. antiquus*

FIG. 27.—A Bark Raft.

with such a spear would have been to add so trifling an injury to such a tremendous insult, that the huge beast would have turned on the hunter with disastrous results; probably the pitfall was the method adopted (p. 57).

We think the illustration in Mr. Crawford's book is the first which has appeared of this Clacton spear. The book itself consists of a series of brilliant essays on the whole Art of Archæology, and should be read by any boy, or girl, who wishes to acquire the proper atmosphere for more detailed study.

The Tasmanians were wonderful trackers, with very acute sight, hearing, and smell.

They ate the animals and birds they caught. Without any preliminaries these were thrown on to a wood fire which singed the hair and feathers and half-cooked the carcase. Then the bodies were cut apart with a flint and gutted, and the cooking finished off by spitting the joints on sticks, and toasting over the fire. A little wood ash served instead of salt. The meat was always roast, because there were not any pots to boil in.

The Tasmanians ate shell-fish as well, and these the women caught by diving into the sea and searching the rocks under water. They had not any nets, hooks, or lines. The women were not treated very well, and had to do all the other work while the men hunted. They sat behind their lords at meals, who, reclining on one arm in Roman fashion, passed the tougher morsels to their dutiful spouses.

The Tasmanians had one notable possession in their raft. This was not hollow like a boat, but made of cigar-shaped rolls of very light bark like cork. One large central roll had two smaller ones lashed to it with grass rope to prevent rolling; see section on Fig. 27; so that it was a raft in canoe shape. With these, or in them, they crossed from headland to headland, and the type may have been a survival of the earlier boats by which their ancestors found their way down from the mainland, and bridged the gaps between the islands, if the isthmus we referred to did not exist.

This raft is of great interest, because at some time or other it must have been a notable development. Pithecanthropus, if he ever went boating, did so on any floating log, and discovered to his disgust that it needed pointing, if it was to be paddled along, and also that some sort of arrangement was necessary to prevent it rolling over in the water, and giving him an involuntary bath. The beginning came in some such way. One development was the dug-out, and certain prehistoric men, with fire and flint, shaped and hollowed their log in this way.

The Tasmanian was another and very much readier method. The rafts were used for fishing, and carried three to four men comfortably; the spear, which was their only fishing implement, served as well for a paddle. A clay floor was made at one end, and here a fire was lighted.

It is difficult for us to realize, with matches at hand, what a precious possession fire was to any primitive people. To obtain it they had to follow the method Darwin saw practised by the Tahitians. "A light was procured by rubbing a blunt-pointed stick in a groove made in another, as if with the intention of deepening it, until by friction the dust became ignited" (Fig. 13). It must have been a difficult business, depending on a supply of dry moss, or fibrous bark, which could be lighted from the dust set on fire by friction. The Tasmanian then carried his fire about with him in the form of decayed touchwood, which would smoulder for hours, and could then be blown into flame.

Everyday Life in the Old Stone Age

They made grass rope and string, by twisting long wiry grass or fibrous bark, as Fig. 28. This illustration is of great interest, in that it leads up to the development of the spinning spindle shown in Fig. 40. Primitive man, of course, used sinews and hide thongs for ties. They also made clumsy reed baskets, and at the British Museum is a water-carrying vessel, made by skewering up the corners of the leaf of a large seaweed kelp. It looks rather like a mob-cap. With a grass rope they climbed high trees. They passed the rope round themselves and the tree; cut holes in the bark for their big toes, first on one side, and then the other, and as they went up, jerked the rope and themselves up the tree together.

It is not known if they had any idea of trade or barter, but they did not grow any crops, or possess any domesticated animals. They were without any overlords, laws, or regular government.

If they ailed, an incision was made in the body, to let the pain escape. The dead were sometimes burned, and sometimes placed in hollow trees. After burning, the remains might be buried, but the skull retained and worn as a memento, or at other times this was buried separately. They believed in a life after death on a pleasant island with their ancestors.

We will finish off this account of the Tasmanians by an amusing description of one of the ways they had of settling their quarrels: "The parties approach one another face to face, and folding their arms across their breasts, shake their heads (which occasionally come in contact) in each other's faces, uttering at the same time the most vociferous and angry expressions, until one or the other is exhausted, or his feelings of anger subside." An extremely sensible method, and amusing for the onlookers, which is more than can be said of civilized methods of quarrelling.

It is not very creditable to the civilized white races, that the Tasmanians should have been used so badly that they have now become extinct. Truganini, the last survivor, died in 1877, and, we hope, found the dream of the pleasant island and the kindly ancestors come true. A nation can die of a broken heart, even as individuals; or shall we say, they lose heart. Think of a people who have supported life with no other aid than spears, waddies, and chipped flints; then other people come in ships, with a wonderful apparatus for living, which makes the sticks and stones seem foolish and inadequate. The old people naturally lose interest and heart, and the desire to go on living, or become hangers-on, and so come to an end. All of which is very sad.

We have written enough to prove that Chellean and Acheulean men, in their flint bouchers, possessed tools with which they could make the spears that they needed to kill game for food; their mode of living must have been very similar to the Tasmanians. Shall we now try to conjure up a picture of a tribe here in England in Chellean and Acheulean times, and find out if we can how they supported life?

The tribe was like a large family in those days. There might have been a headman, who would have been the boldest of the hunters, but little if any system of government. The women did all the work, and looked after the children, and meant more to them than the father, whose place was with the hunters. So much was this the case that custom grew up in savage races of tracing descent on the mother's side.

The tribe would not have been particularly quarrelsome, unless their neighbours trespassed on their hunting-grounds. War is a civilized institu-

8.—Making Grass Rope.

Fɪɢ. 30.—Neanderthaler or Mousterian.

ɪɢ. 31.—Poise of the
Mousterian Figure.

Fɪɢ. 33.—Mouster-
ian Spear-head.

tion, based as a rule on the desire to obtain some other nation's property. Prehistoric man had little temptation in this way. Our tribe may have camped on the banks of the Wey for the summer. The river was a much bigger one than it is now, and one hopes they found the fishing good. In any case they would only have had the wooden spear to lance the fish with, and a flint boucher to cut it up afterwards. There would have been berries to eat, the roots of bracken and ferns, and nuts in the autumn, crab apples, wild cherries, and sloes. The bee had to give up his store to greedy hands that tore the comb, and crunched it up without waiting to run out the honey. There were snails and shell-fish, grubs and beetles, and luscious caterpillars.

Greatest joy of all a dead elephant, or hippo, or perhaps a rhinoceros, then would the tribe have sat down, and eaten their way through the carcase; if it happened to be a little bit high, we need not sniff, because we still like pheasant in the same condition.

But rough plenty would not last; hard times and winter would come on, and the tribe range far and wide in search of food. They would grow lean-ribbed as wolves, and just as savage. They would be driven by hunger to attack living game, and in the fight some would die that the others might live. The survivors at the meal would not have presented a pleasant spectacle; they would have torn the beast to pieces, and eaten it raw.

It must have been a hard life, yet the Call of the Wild still takes the big-game hunter to Africa, and the explorer to Polar Regions. The sick and ailing went to the wall, because little could be done for them. If a tooth ached, it continued to do so, until it stopped of its own accord. Chellean man did not practise dentistry. Notwithstanding all this, he was not a degraded savage, because this means a falling from high estate. He possessed the soul which makes man the restless individual that he still is. Just as the inventor of to-day has conquered the air, and seeks to harness all the powers of nature, so Chellean man experimented with his chipped flints, and found out the way to support life. There were doubtless good, bad, and indifferent men, as there are now; some who push the world along, and others who retard its progress, but whether he hated, loved, hunted, or fought, our ancestor was fighting our battles as well as his own, and through all the thousands of years slowly struggling on an upward path.

Strepyan, Chellean, Acheulean Men

NOTE.—In the limited space of this chapter, we have not been able to write much as to the actual manufacture of flint implements, or show the infinite variety of their shapes. At the British Museum, in the Prehistoric Room, in one of the table cases, there is a series of flints arranged to explain their manufacture, and in the cases of the Gallery over, a collection of magnificent specimens. If readers are interested, they should pay a visit to Bloomsbury, or to the County Museums which have collections. A sight of the actual implements will make our pages more real.

CHAPTER III

OUR next period is that of the Cave-dwellers, or Mousterians, so called after the cave of Le Moustier, in the valley of the Vézère, Dordogne (Fig. 29). Here again we are indebted to the French archæologists, who have examined the prehistoric remains so carefully that we have had to adopt their names. At Le Moustier, the river has in course of time cut its way down through the limestone, which is left in cliff formation at the sides. In the cliffs, caverns were formed by surface water finding its way down from the top and wearing away pockets of softer stone, or by the river cutting out holes in the banks. This left the caves ready for the occupation of man, and, as the weather became colder, he looked about and found ready-made houses, a thing we should like to do to-day. When prehistoric man first inhabited these, they were just above the flood-level of the river; to-day they are often high up on the banks,

92

FIG. 29.—Mousterian Cave-dwellers.

The Cave-Dwellers

because the river has continued to cut out its bed. All along the Vézère are caves, which are known all the world over by archæologists, and later on we shall hear of La Madeleine, La Micoque, Crô-Magnon, and others.

We will start by considering Mousterian man. In 1907, a skeleton was discovered in a cave on the banks of the Sourdoire, a tributary of the Dordogne, in the district of La Chapelle aux Saints. Let us at once point out that this is the first time we have found any evidence of people burying their dead in a place of sepulchre. The Piltdown man, and his cousin of Java, the man of Heidelberg, just dropped in their tracks, were brought down by the river currents, settled into the mud, and were covered up by gravel. In the case of the man of La Chapelle aux Saints, it is evident that he had been buried with care and perhaps love. Flint implements were laid ready to his hand for use in the hunting-grounds of the spirit world, and food for his sustenance. Think of the difference this means in the mental outlook of the relatives, and regard it as a notable step up the ladder of civilization. A similar discovery was also made at Le Moustier in 1908.

Everyday Life in the Old Stone Age

These discoveries were very important, because they enabled the archæologists to be quite sure of their facts in respect to other skeletons which had been found. In 1857, a specimen was discovered in a limestone cave at Neanderthal, near Düsseldorf, Germany; unfortunately, as in the case of the Piltdown man, the workmen who found it, not realizing its value, broke up the skeleton. Remember the Java man was not discovered until 1891, and the Piltdown man in 1912, so the scientists were not prepared for the Neanderthaler in '57. Some said the latter individual must have suffered from "something on the brain," to have had such an extraordinary shape to his head, but Huxley the great Englishman and others recognized the skull as human. From time to time various other skulls were found, until that of La Chapelle aux Saints confirmed the opinion that all belonged to one race, which is called the Neanderthal or Mousterian (*Homo Neanderthalensis*).

Our drawing (Fig. 30) shows what these men looked like, and has been made from the casts of the skulls of the Neanderthal and La Chapelle aux Saints men at the Natural History Museum. The most noticeable characteristic of the Mousterian

FIG. 32.—Mousterians on the March.

The Cave-Dwellers

skull is the one very *prominent* ridge going right across the brows. The frontal bones are very thick, and there is not much chin to the lower jaw. The head is large in proportion to the height, and the shin and thigh bones suggest that the man stood with knees bent forward a little (see Fig. 31). The arm, again, is longer than that of modern man. It should be noticed that the head is placed on the shoulders in quite a different way to ours. If any of our readers stand with bent knees, they will find that the head and shoulders swing forward. Mousterian man must have loped along, head to ground like a hunting animal, and would have found it difficult to look up (Fig. 32).

Mousterian man was widely distributed, and though he seems to have been the first to use the cave, he did not entirely desert the camping-places of his ancestors on the river banks. He is supposed to have lived at the end of the Fourth Glacial period, so perhaps, as the weather gradually became warmer, he spent some of his summers on the Somme. Here M. Commont has identified his implements in the Ergeron, or younger Loess, which, as we have seen, was deposited by wind on the terraces.

Everyday Life in the Old Stone Age

The boucher disappeared soon after the beginning of the Mousterian period; this in Acheulean times was made by knocking flakes off a nodule of flint. The flakes were used for making small scrapers and the like. Mousterian man appears to have dressed one side of his implement first on the nodule, and then to have detached it as a large flake. This, again, is an interesting fact, and shows that man was beginning to economize in the use of material. The weather too was becoming colder, and the hills would have been covered with snow. Flint is only found in chalk of the cretaceous beds. In many parts of the country it has all been cut away by the action of water, and the flints taken with it to form gravel in the river terraces lower down. Flint suitable for making implements must have been valuable to prehistoric man, and a stray flint from the surface is not so good for flaking as one quarried out of chalk. So for some it meant a long journey, and encounters with woolly rhinoceros *en route*, to obtain the raw material for his industry, then perhaps the bartering of skins in exchange for the flints, and a toilsome carrying home of the heavy stones. Perhaps it occurred to Mousterian man that if instead of wasting a whole large flint to make one boucher, he used the flakes, he could make several implements out of one nodule. This is what he did, and it marks one more step up the ladder.

We call these Levallois flakes. Sharp-pointed flints are also found notched on one side, evidently for use as lance-heads (Fig. 33).

Spherical balls of limestone have been found, and it is thought that these may have been used as bolas. Darwin describes the bolas used by the Gauchos of Monte Video, South America. "The bolas, or balls, are of two kinds. The simplest, which is chiefly used for catching ostriches, consists of two round stones covered with leather and untied by a thin plaited thong about eight feet long; the other kind differs only in having three balls untied by thongs to a common centre. The Gaucho holds the smallest of the three in his hand, and whirls the other two round and round his head; then, taking aim, sends them like chain shot revolving through the air. The balls no sooner strike any object than, winding round it, they cross each other and become firmly hitched." The Gaucho lives on horseback, but the Eskimo goes on foot, and he uses a bolas with seven or eight cords, and attached stones, and this he uses to bring down birds on the wing. The stones are formed by being knocked together till they become round.

The Reindeer and Musk Ox were newcomers from the north in Mousterian times, and were hunted by prehistoric man for his food; but we do not find anything that would lead us to suppose that he had as yet domesticated animals.

There is one very black mark against the Mousterians, and that is evidence, which is supposed to point to cannibalism, contained in deposits in the Rock Shelter of Krapina, in Croatia. Here were found human bones which had been broken, as if to extract the marrow, and burnt by fire. It appears that the Australian aborigines, while not being habitual cannibals, yet practised this dreadful art, as a ceremonial way of disposing of the dead bodies of their relatives.

It will be seen from the foregoing that, though we know a little more about the Mousterians than about Chellean and Acheulean man, it does not amount to very much. We must search for some primitive people living under similar conditions, and at about the same stage of civilization as the

FIG. 34.—Australian Spear-throwing.

FIG. 38.—Making Fire.

FIG. 35.—Australian Spear-throwing.

The Cave-Dwellers

Mousterians, and see if we can draw useful comparisons. The aborigines of Australia are such a people. Of them Messrs. Spencer and Gillen have written that they "have no idea of permanent abodes, no clothing, no knowledge of any implements save those fashioned out of wood, bone, and stone, no idea whatever of the cultivation of crops, or of the laying in of a supply of food to tide over hard times, no word for any number beyond three, and no belief in anything like a supreme being." They have not been treated quite so brutally as the Tasmanians were, and are still allowed to exist on sufferance, and end their days as a race on the unfertile lands. In the beginning, it seems as if they followed the Tasmanians into Australia from the mainland, and settled there, driving some of the latter people into Tasmania and mixing with them to some extent.

The scientists divide mankind into three groups: the Cymotrichi, with wavy hair like ourselves, and the Australians, come into this group; the Lissotrichi, whose hair is perfectly straight, like that of the Eskimo; the Ulotrichi, whose hair is very twisted, as in the case of the Negroes, Bushmen, and Tasmanians. Their spear shows a considerable development on that of the Tasmanians, and resembles the Mousterian type. About ten feet long, some have hardwood points on to which barbs were spliced; others a flint point, as Fig. 33. The Australians use a spear-thrower. This has many forms, but the essential feature is a stick about a yard long, with a handle at one end, and a peg at the other. Figs. 34 and 35 show the spear-thrower in use. First the end of the spear is fitted on to the peg of the thrower. This is held in the right hand well behind the body, the left hand balancing the spear. It is then thrown up and forward, the thrower imparting an additional impulse as the spear leaves the hand. Darwin when in Australia saw the natives at practice. He wrote: "A cap being fixed at thirty yards distance, they transfixed it with a spear, delivered by the throwing-stick with the rapidity of an arrow from the bow of a practised archer."

This short range means that the Australian must be an expert hunter and tracker, if he is to approach within striking distance of his quarry, the kangaroo. Mousterian spear-throwers have not been discovered in Europe as yet, but we can safely assume that the shorter type, as Fig. 67, which is a

Fig. 37.—Australian Hut.

harpoon-thrower, was not arrived at without many simpler forms going before. The Australian uses a wooden shield, which is a development on the Tasmanian equipment. Very much narrower than those of mediæval times, it is a long oval in shape, varying from 2 feet to 2 feet 6 inches in length, by 6 to 12 inches in width. Rounded on the outside, the inside of the shield is hollowed out so as to leave a vertical handle. When one thinks that this is all cut out of the solid with a flint, it becomes a notable piece of work. The shield points to quarrels and fighting, because its only purpose can be to protect the user against spear thrusts. We do not know if the Mousterian used shields.

Before we forget it, let us say that our readers should pay a visit to the Ethnographical Gallery at the British Museum, and see there a spear-head made by the Australians, in recent times, from broken bottle glass; it is an astonishing production, and the man who made it a great craftsman. A visit should be paid to the British Room where there are Mousterian types, and so comparisons can be drawn.

The Australians make very useful knives out of long dagger-shaped flakes of stone, and by daubing resin at one end form rounded handles. They mount sharp flakes in the ends of sticks with resin, and these are used as chisels and adzes. There are stone picks inserted like the spear-heads in cleft sticks, only at right angles; these were secured with tendons and resin. Stone axes are made, and these are hafted in a withy handle, made supple by heat, and then bent around the axe, and fastened with tendons and resin. This suggests that the flaked stone found by Mr. Falkner at Churt, near Farnham, Surrey (Fig. 36), may have been mounted in much the same way.

The Australian implements should be seen at the British Museum. Some of their work is ground and polished, and here in Europe we associate this with the next period, the Neolithic. Their methods of hafting are of great interest, and prehistoric people must also have used some such way to protect their hands from the razor-like edges of the flints. Like the Tasmanians, the Australians walk abroad without any clothes, but wear skin cloaks in their huts; they stitch these together with sinew, and use bone awls and pins for piercing the skins. Necklaces and forehead bands of shells and teeth are worn, and they make themselves beautiful by

Fig. 39.—A Bark Canoe.

pushing a short stick, called a nose-pin, through the thin membrane which divides the nostrils. They also sacrifice joints of their little fingers, as we shall find the Aurignacians did in Europe. Their huts are very simple, and serve for the camp of a day or so, which makes a break in their wanderings. Fig. 37 shows such a type, which may have been used by Mousterian man in the summer when he left his cave. It represents the next development that we should expect from the Tasmanian's break-wind (Fig. 22). It is, in fact, like two break-winds leaning together, and was made of any rough branches that came to hand.

The Australians have another method of lighting fires by friction: one stick is held in the hands and rotated in a hole in another, until the wood dust is ignited (Fig. 38). Darwin gives an improvement on this method: "the Gaucho in the Pampas . . . taking an elastic stick about eighteen inches long, presses one end on his breast, and the other pointed end into a hole in a piece of wood, then rapidly turns the curved part like a carpenter's centre-bit."

Another interesting development is the bark canoe of the Australians, as Fig. 39. The lines of this are much the same as that of the Tasmanians (Fig. 27), but the construction is that of a real boat, not a raft. A long strip of bark is stripped from the gum tree with a stone axe and warmed over a fire to make it supple. Curved saplings, bent as ribs, give the shape, and a stretcher goes across the tops of these, and the boat is prevented from spreading by grass rope ties from side to side. The prow and stern are tied up with stringy bark. A small fire is carried on a clay floor. The Australians are great fishermen and have invented a barbed harpoon, and fish-hooks of shell and wood.

The point of the comparison is that in Europe, after Mousterian times, we come across well-made harpoons, which could only have been used for fishing. These could not have developed without long experiment. Mousterian man may have gone fishing with a spear without barbs, and from his poor catches may have thought out the more effective harpoon. Therefore, they must have used some form of canoe, which, of course, has long since disappeared, so we turn to another primitive people for inspiration. The Australians make another form of canoe where bark is sewn on to the framework. The coracle of Wales and Ireland,

114

The Cave-Dwellers

the kayak and umiak of the Eskimo, were of this form, only skins were used instead of bark, and this may have been the Mousterian method. We do know that in Europe in Neolithic times the dug-out canoe was employed.

The Australians carry on trade by barter. The red ochre they need for decorating their bodies, may be exchanged for stone suitable for making implements. They have not any form of writing, but send news about by message sticks. There is one in the British Museum from North Queensland. It resembles a short wooden lath about three inches long, with zigzag cuts and notches. The meaning of the message is "that the dogs are being properly cared for, and that the writer wants clothes." The lady would not have worn more than a skin cloak, with perhaps a hair fringe round her waist, and a necklace of shells, so that her dress allowance would not have needed to be very considerable. We do not hear the husband's reply, but expect it was that he was short of the equivalent of cash. The Australians are excellent hunters, as were the Tasmanians. Kangaroos are eaten, also almost all the other animals and birds, grubs and the pupæ of ants, fish and shell-

Everyday Life in the Old Stone Age

fish. Their cooking is very much like that of the Tasmanians, the animals, being first gutted, are cooked in a pit. All tendons are removed for use.

Another notable development is that the women collect the seeds of various grasses and plants, and grind these down between stones and winnow by pouring from one *pitchi* into another, so that the husks are blown away. They make rough cakes of the resulting flour. The *pitchi* is a shallow wooden trough used for shovel or scoop as well. The Mousterians may have collected seeds in the same way, and so have started the long chain which led up to the household loaf of to-day. The Australian women use a yam or digging-stick, like the one illustrated (Fig. 62), but not loaded with a stone to increase weight. The yam-stick is not used to cultivate the soil, but for digging up honey, ants or lizards which are eaten. Remember, we have seen that Darwin found people living exclusively on meat, and that this was general before the advent of agriculture; but this collecting of seeds would naturally have suggested the idea of growing plants for food.

The Australians did not practise cannibalism, except in a ceremonial way, when, as is the case in

The Cave-Dwellers

Victoria, they regarded it as a reverent method of disposing of dead relatives.

We have seen that the Tasmanians made rush baskets, and grass rope for climbing trees and tying up their rafts. With the rope they would have learned the principle of twisting together short lengths of fibre, so that these made a continuous string. This is the principle of all spinning. The wool with which the stockings of our readers are darned is in reality a number of short hairs kept in shape by the twist of the spindle of the spinning machine. Fray out an inch of wool and see. The Arunta tribes in Central Australia can manufacture twine of fur or human hair. For this they use a spindle as A (shown in Fig. 40): this is a stick about fourteen inches long which at the spinning end is pushed through holes in two thin curved sticks, about six inches long, placed at right angles to one another. Some fur or hair is pulled out, and part of it twisted with the finger into a thread long enough to be tied on to the end of the spindle; this is rotated by being rubbed up or down the thigh. The remainder of the fur held in the hand is allowed to be drawn out as the spindle twists the thread; this is then wound up on to the spindle, and more of the fur paid out, and more thread twisted. This, we think, is the greatest achievement of the Australians, and they, as we have seen, are to all intents and purposes living in a Stone Age. The problem is, for how long they have used the spindle; did they bring it with them in remote ages from the mainland; did prehistoric man, whom the Australians so closely resemble, use a spindle? They must have needed rope, and if they made it in this way, then the sixteenth-century spinning-wheel, and the eighteenth-century spinning-jenny, would have their roots very deep in the past, because both are only mechanically driven spindles which trace their descent from something like Fig. 40. The Australian does not use his twine for weaving, but contents himself with making net bags. Fig. 28 shows a still more primitive method of making twine out of long shreds of bark.

The Australians have a very complicated system of relationship. A group will be divided into two classes or phratries: one-half may be Crows, the other Lizards. A Crow would marry a Lizard, not another Crow; would be kind to all the other Crows, and regard the birds of that name as feath-

The Cave-Dwellers

ered friends. This was a means not only of bind-
ing men together in fellowship and friendship, but
it preserved the decencies, and prevented the
marriage of persons too closely related for it to
be seemly. Each group had various ceremonies,
generally concerned with invoking the totem
animal to promote plenty. In Aurignacian times
in Europe, it is suggested that the cave paintings
may have had totemic significance. Totemism is
very widely spread, and gives us a new respect for
primitive peoples; it shows them shaping their
lives to a system, and not just chattering their way
along like so many monkeys.

The Australians have not any other settled form
of government, but each group or tribe has a headman, who by reason of skill in hunting or special
gifts takes the lead. They are not a quarrelsome
people. War is a terrible luxury in which primitive man cannot afford to indulge. His quarrels
were mere skirmishes as to boundaries of hunting-
grounds; it never occurs to the Australian to steal
his neighbour's territory. In his opinion this is
inhabited by the spirits of their ancestors, and so
would be a useless possession to him.

The Australians very frequently associate death

not with natural causes, but with magic wrought by an enemy. This leads to trouble, because if the medicine man of the tribe names the enemy, and the enemy is a neighbour, he is tracked down and put to death. In this way, the unfortunate native helps to bring about his own extinction. This fear of magic has always been strong in the minds of primitive people.

Games of all sorts are played by the children, who practise throwing spears, and also an amusing little implement called the "weet-weet," because it has the form of a kangaroo rat. Then a day comes when the boys are grown up, and are initiated and become men. Dances are performed by the men before the novitiates to typify essential qualities. The dog and kangaroo are shown for endurance and speed. The boy has one of his front teeth knocked out to teach him to bear pain. The bull roarer, a long flat leaf-shaped piece of wood scored across, is whirled round on a thong, and the whistling noise it makes is thought to be the voice of a god. It is the boy's introduction to the spiritual life of the tribe; to a knowledge of the Mysteries, and of the High God who lives in the Sky.

The Cave-Dwellers

When an Australian is born it is assumed that he brings with him a *churinga;* these are long flat pieces of wood or stone with rounded ends, marked with various totem devices, and considered sacred objects. These are deposited in caves, and only brought out for ceremonies.

The Australians have various methods of disposing of their dead, but burial is the most general. With the bodies are interred weapons, food, and a drinking-cup for use in the happy hunting-grounds, so that in one more detail they resemble the Mousterian man of La Chapelle aux Saints, with whose remains a flint boucher was found.

We need not continue these comparisons, but we hope that those we have given may help to build up a picture of what the surroundings of Mousterian man may have been like.

At the end of the second chapter we gave a sketch of Chellean man, and tried to show that his most urgent need was food; that unless he hunted, he starved, and could not depend, as we do, on a shop round the corner, and the effort of other men. This was the material side of his life; but what of the spiritual? We shall be quite wrong if we think of primitive man as being only concerned with food, because man has always demanded some other interest.

We have the very early belief in a life hereafter, in the happy hunting-grounds, where conditions were kindlier, and there was more opportunity to expand. The Chapelle aux Saints burial, with flint implements to hand, for use in the spirit world, points to this. How did this come about? Primitive man, or woman, curled round asleep by his fire, dreamed dreams and saw visions; his spirit seemed to separate from his body, and he joined old friends who were dead, and with them followed in the chase, or did the wonderful things we all do in our dreams. When he awakened and rubbed sleepy eyes to find his own fireside, he told his friends of his adventures; that so and so was not dead, but a spirit in a wonderful world. We can see the beginnings of ancestor worship. An acute fit of indigestion, coming after too much mammoth, would have provided the nightmare, and its equivalent horrors, and an underworld of bad spirits.

The man of imagination would have polished up the tale, and filled in the gaps, and gaining much renown thereby, he became the medicine man

The Cave-Dwellers

or priest. He would exorcise the evil spirits, for a consideration, or bring messages from the good ones. At other times, in the excitement of hunting, the voice of the man would be echoed back from the hills, where by search he could find no other people. It was magical and mysterious, just as it was when his own face looked back at him from the pool to which he stooped to drink.

The sun, moon, and stars gave him cause for wonder, and glaciers mightier than the Baltoro seemed to him alive, as they crept to the sea. He made them gods. Perhaps on a stormy day he looked through a rift in the clouds, and saw others heaped and peaked into glittering pinnacles lighted by a sun he could not see himself, and thought of it all as the pleasant country of the land of dreams. The long nights and storms made him fearful.

We can never know very much about the poor Mousterian, because, most sadly to relate, at the end of the Fourth Glacial period he became extinct in Europe. He had done as much as was possible for him. His large head, with the thick frontal bones, must have been very good for butting a brother Neanderthaler, but it was no use against the stone wall of advancing civilization, and like the Tasmanian and Bushman, the Red Indian and Australian of nowadays, he fades out of the picture, and his place is taken by a cleverer people.

CHAPTER IV

AURIGNACIAN MAN

WITH Mousterian man the Lower Palæolithic period of the Old Stone Age came to an end, and the next phase we shall consider will be the Upper Palæolithic. At the base of this we find the Aurignacian or Loess men, and of these there are at least three types. Fig. 41 shows the Crô-Magnon, and is a sufficient explanation why the poor old Neanderthaler or Mousterian went to the wall.

The Crô-Magnon man gains his name because his remains were found in a rock shelter of that name in the valley of the Vézère; the same river which has the cave of Le Moustier on its banks (p. 92). The bodies had evidently been buried with reverence and were probably clothed. Flint implements for use in the spirit world were found with the skeletons. The Crô-Magnon people were a

125

fine race, with an average height of six feet. The skulls are dolichocephalic, cephalic index 73.41, well shaped with a capacity of 1590 to 1715 cubic centimetres, quite up to the average to-day. The faces were broad and the chin well developed. Man's jaw was the last thing to be civilized. Our drawing (Fig. 41) has been made from the plaster casts at the British Museum, and shows a type which can be recognized as modern man (*Homo sapiens*).

The second type (Fig. 42) was discovered in 1909 at Combe Capelle, on the Couze, a tributary of the Dordogne. The body, when buried, had been provided with flint implements, and perforated shells were found which had probably been used to decorate the clothing. The skull is very long and narrow, and the skeleton that of a man of short stature, in contrast to the Crô-Magnon, who was tall.

An Aurignacian skeleton has been found in this country at Paviland, in South Wales.

At the same time there appears to have been a third type, the Grimaldi, in Europe during Aurignacian times (Fig. 43). Skeletons have been found at the Grotte des Enfants at Mentone, which

FIG. 42.—Combe Capelle Man.

FIG. 41.—The Crô-Magnon Man.

FIG. 43.—Grimaldi Man.

FIG. 45.—The Spokeshave.

show marked differences to the Crô-Magnon man. The skulls are dolichocephalic, but the mouth projected in a prognathous manner, with the chin retreating under. The nose was flat and of negroid character; the people not more than 5 feet to 5 feet 6 inches in height. Prof. Sollas, in his book *Ancient Hunters*, reviews the evidence which points to these people as the ancestors of the Bushmen of South Africa; they may, in fact, have first come from Africa, and then have been forced back by the cleverer Crô-Magnons. The Aurignacians were cave-dwellers but lived as well in the open; their camps have been found in the newer Loess and for this reason they have been called the Loess Men. If, as has been thought, the Bushmen may be the descendants of the Aurignacians, we may perhaps assume that the Loess men had the same sort of huts. These the Bushmen constructed, much as the gipsy does to-day with a frame-work of bent sticks covered with skins (Fig. 44). Darwin wrote of the "toldos" of the Indians near Bahia Blanca, South America, "these are round like ovens, and covered with hides; by the mouth of each a tapering chuzo (spear) was stuck in the ground."

Everyday Life in the Old Stone Age

The Aurignacian people improved on the Mousterian flint implements; we find several sorts of scrapers, knives, and gravers; the latter a tool for engraving of which they made very clever use. There are scrapers flaked ingeniously into very useful spokeshaves, and Fig. 45 shows a man shaving down the shaft for a lance. The Aurignacian man, judged by the variety of tools which he possessed, must have been a clever workman making all sorts of things; remember all his woodwork has disappeared, and we only find now the imperishable flint, and some bone implements. With his burin, or graving tool he easily cut pieces out of reindeer horns, and made arrow and spear heads. This use of bone marks another step forward, and from now on we shall find many examples of this new material. Bone bodkins were used to pierce skins and pass sinews through, then the bodkin had a blunt barb formed at one end to pull the thong through like a crochet-needle, and so led up to the bone needles of Upper Solutrean times later on (Fig. 52). Later on we shall find barbed harpoons. The Aurignacian used the bow and arrow—we know this because shaft-straighteners have been found, bored to take shafts of different thicknesses.

Fig. 44.—Type of Huts suggested by Aurignacian drawings.

Artists of the Old Stone Age

These were used as shown in Fig. 46. The shaft, after having been shaved clean, would have been passed over a wood fire to make it supple, and then slipped through the hole of the shaft-straightener, which is cut obliquely. It can be seen that pressure applied on the handle would bend the shaft in any desired direction. The natives of the Punjab in India still straighten bamboos in this way, only their shaft-straightener is a substantial post set strongly in the ground. Through this there are bored holes, and the warmed bamboo is put through these, and curves removed by bending the stem in an opposite direction. The Eskimo, on the other hand, follows the Aurignacian way. The early bow, like the early gun, was probably not very effective, and the spear must have remained the great weapon. Darwin, writing of the Indians from the south of Chile, said: "The only weapon of an Indian is a very long bamboo or chuzo, ornamented with ostrich feathers, and pointed by a sharp spear-head." The boring of holes in the shaft-straightener, and the use of the bow, suggests that the Aurignacians used the bow-drill both to bore holes and make fire, as the Eskimos do (Fig. 47).

Everyday Life in the Old Stone Age

The Aurignacians hunted as the Mousterians had done for their food, and people had not yet learned how to domesticate animals, or grow food-stuffs. The reindeer were very plentiful; so much is this the case that the French archæologists talk of the Upper Palæolithic as the Age of the Reindeer. The climate was improving, and as the Fourth Glacial period receded, game became more plentiful. The horse was eaten in those days, and in France huge mounds of the bones have been discovered, left as the débris of many Aurignacian feasts. Even so late as 1831, Darwin wrote of South American troops: "Mare's flesh is the only food which the soldiers have when on an expedition."

Here is an account of how the horses may have been caught, taken from Falconer's *Patagonia:* "The Indians drive troops of wild horses into a 'Corral' encompassed by high cliffs between thirty and forty feet high, excepting at one spot where the entrance lies. This is guarded to keep them secure."

In our part of the country, at Ivinghoe Beacon, is a curious cleft in the hills, which tradition says was a wolf trap in olden days, and its form cer-

FIG. 46.—Shaft-straightening.

FIG. 47.—The Bow drill.

FIG. 48.—*Cervus giganteus*, the Irish Deer.

tainly lends to it the appearance of a corral. There appears to have been plenty of food in Aurignacian times. Fig. 48 has been drawn from the skeleton of the Irish Deer (*Cervus giganteus*) in the Natural History Museum. This splendid animal was found in Europe during Pleistocene times.

There is another fact which goes to show that the conditions of life were becoming easier. Man and perhaps woman began to draw, and to do so extremely well. This is a most interesting fact, and one which should be noted, that the tribe was content to let these people spend their time in this way. One can imagine that the Mousterian or Neanderthaler, very much occupied with the struggle for existence at the end of the Fourth Glacial period, would have dealt sternly with the budding artist, who desired to cut his share of the "chores," because he wanted to draw; but in Aurignacian times he was allowed to do so, and drawing and sculpture extended into the Magdalenian period. These drawings and paintings are something altogether beyond the art of ordinary savage people. The Australians, for instance, decorate their wooden shields with red, white, and black, wavy lines, and lozenges, which have a pleasantly decorative effect;

but of the polychrome figures which marked the culmination of Magdalenian art, the Abbé Breuil has written: "Et qui place les vieux peintres des âges glyptiques bien au-dessus des animaliers de toutes les civilizations de l'orient classique et de la Grèce." So here is another problem; it is quite certain that endless experiment must have been made before the artists could have arrived at such marvellous dexterity. How did these wonderful people jump out of the void of time? These drawings were first discovered by a Spanish nobleman, Marcellino de Santuola, who lived at Santander, Spain. He was interested in archæology and was digging one day in the cave of Altamira, near his home. With him was his little daughter, who, tired of watching the digging, wandered round the cave, and alarmed her father by calling out "Toros! Toros!" Bulls in a cave would be somewhat alarming, and M. Santuola, hurrying to the rescue, found the small girl gazing at the roof of the cavern. Here he discovered drawings and paintings of bulls, bison, deer, horses, and many other animals, some life size. The discovery threw the archæological world into commotion—most discoveries do; people could not believe that these really wonderful

FIG. 49.—Aurignacian Drawing.

drawings could have been produced at such an early stage in the world's history. Just as the Neanderthaler was not at first believed to be a man, and the Eoliths are not yet generally recognized as the work of man, so the Altamira drawings were received with scepticism. That stage has been passed through now, many books have been written, innumerable papers read before learned societies, and other drawings discovered in certain French caves, which have convinced the archæologists that in the Altamira cave are authentic works of the earliest period of the world's art; and we owe the discovery to one small girl who called "Toros!" in alarm to her father.

The old painters seem to have started with drawings in outline like Fig. 49, and then later in Magdalenian times they passed on to colour (as Fig. 1), and some of these have an engraved outline. If our readers are interested, they should try and see a book by the Abbé Breuil, a distinguished Frenchman who has made a special study of this work.

We must pass on to a consideration of what purpose the drawings served. At Altamira, they are in a dark cave, which has a total length of 280 metres; and a metre is about 3 feet 3⅜ inches.

Everyday Life in the Old Stone Age

There is no light in the cave, and the figures occur over all the walls. They cannot be seen now without a light, and a lamp must have been used when they were painted; so we have another discovery, that man had artificial illumination in Aurignacian times. A dark cave, though, does not make a good picture gallery for display, and it does not seem as if the Cave were the National Galley of the day.

Many suggestions have been made as to the uses of the paintings; one is that as most of the animals drawn are those which were hunted for food, the paintings formed a magic which placed the animals under the power of the medicine man of the tribe. Many of the animals are drawn with arrows sticking in their bodies; on some the heart is shown in red. This was a practice which lingered on till recent times—to make a model of your enemy and stick it full of pins; that is, if you were a spiteful person and wished him harm.

The Aurignacians were accomplished sculptors and modelled quite good little figures in the round about four to five inches high, and as well in low relief. A curious detail is that the faces are not rendered; in their drawings and paintings, they seldom if ever presented the human figure, except

142

occasionally by grotesque faces. This may have arisen from the fact that primitive people think that a picture or figure of a man becomes part of his personality. If damage be done to it, then it reacts on the man, so any recognizable portrait of an individual doubles his risks. In the case of the animals drawn this was desirable to the Aurignacian.

Another suggestion is that the mammoth, the bison, or any of the animals drawn, might have been the Totem of the tribe; that they were grouped in clans, as the brothers of the bison perhaps. This, as we have seen, was a practice with the Australians, the Red Indians of America, and the boy scouts of to-day. The Altamira cave in this case would have been the temple in which were preserved totem symbols. One peculiarity at Altamira is that one drawing is frequently found made on the top of another. The interiors of the loftier caves must have first turned men's ideas in the direction of fine building; something which should be nobler than their little huts, and suitable for ceremonies. Imagine prehistoric man first finding his way into a cave, from the lofty roof of which hung down stalactites, like pendants to the

Everyday Life in the Old Stone Age

fan vaulting of Henry the Seventh's Chapel at Westminster. The stalagmites like rising columns, and all the glittering points would have thrown back the light of his lamp. The cave originated the idea of building which we shall see later as Picts' houses, and at first must have been used as the tribal temples. In the painted caves of France and Spain are found the imprints of hands. A hand has evidently been smeared with colour, and then printed on to the surface of the rock or the hand placed there first, and then colour dusted over it, leaving a white silhouette when the hand was removed. Many of the hands show traces of mutilation; that is, the end of a finger has been cut off at the joint. This dismal practice was widely spread and lasted until recent times. It was a form of sacrifice. It existed among the Australians, the Bushmen of South Africa, and some of the Red Indians, for example, and was practised for a variety of causes, generally as a sign of grief, and to implore the better favour of the gods in future. It seems reasonable, then, to suppose that the Aurignacian people lost the fingers, which must have been so useful to them, in some such way.

The Aurignacian women, and perhaps the men

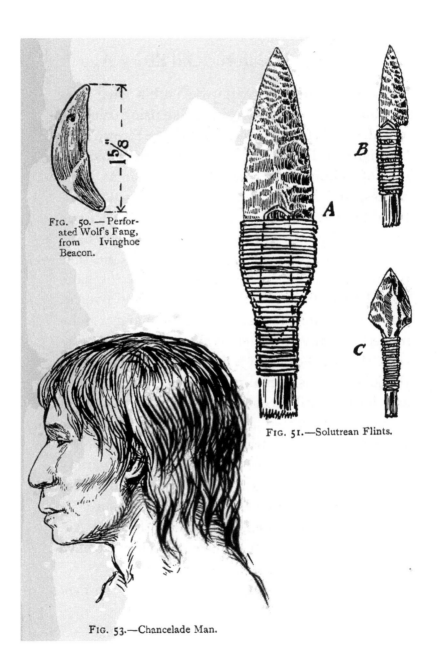

Fig. 50. — Perforated Wolf's Fang, from Ivinghoe Beacon.

1⅝"

A

B

C

Fig. 51.—Solutrean Flints.

Fig. 53.—Chancelade Man.

as well, appear to have been fond of trying to make themselves beautiful. Here in Great Britain, at Paviland Cave in Wales, were found perforated wolves' teeth for use as a necklace, and an ivory bracelet made by sawing rings through the hollow base of a mammoth's tusk. Fig. 50 shows a wolf's tooth from Ivinghoe Beacon. We can also be quite sure that so gifted a people as the Aurignacians must have experimented in the production of music. We know that they had bows and arrows. The twang of the bow led to our piano. The latter is only a harp on its side, the strings of which are struck with hammers instead of plucked with the fingers, and the harp is the bow with many strings; the reed and pipe would lead to the horn, and the drum has always been the great instrument of the native musician. At Alpera, in Spain, are some wonderful paintings of late Palæolithic date, and here are shown figures of women who seem to be dancing. Now dancing means some sort of music, and the cheerful tum-tum of a drum is almost necessary if one is to keep time. In the original Alpera drawings are figures which appear to be wearing quaint head-dresses; perhaps this was a masquerade. If all this sounds improbable, remember their wonderful drawings; to such people much is possible. Dancing has always been an accomplishment of savage people. Darwin wrote of a "corrobery," or dancing party, of the aborigines in Australia, held at night by the light of fires, the women and children squatting round as spectators. An "Emu dance, in which each man extended his arm in a bent manner, like the neck of that bird. In another dance, one man imitated the movements of a kangaroo grazing in the woods whilst a second crawled up and pretended to spear him." In this way they dramatized their everyday life.

SOLUTREAN MAN

The next division of the Upper Palæolithic is the one which the archæologists have named the Solutrean, after Solutré, near Macon (Saône-et-Loire) in France. Solutrean man appears to have lived in England because evidences of his industry have been found at Paviland Cave in South Wales, and Cresswell Crags, Derbyshire; as well as in France, Central Europe, and the North of Spain, but not in Italy. The Solutreans may have been

FIG. 52.—Making of Bone Needles.

horse hunters who invaded Europe along the open grasslands of the Loess. It has been assumed that they were a warlike race, because of the very beautiful flint lance-heads which have been found; some of these are like an assegai, and would have been deadly weapons (Fig. 51). They are beautifully flaked flints, shaped like a laurel leaf, from which they get their name (*pointe en feuille de laurier*); the smaller types like a willow leaf, and so called (*pointe en feuille de saule*). B shows the highest Palæolithic development of flint flaking, the *pointe à cran*, or shouldered point, by which a primitive barb was formed. C is an arrow-head with a flint tang which could be bound on to the shaft.

Flint flaking came to its highest point of development in the Old Stone Age in Solutrean times, though it was to revive again later in the New Stone, or Neolithic Age. The Solutreans made borers, scrapers, and arrow-heads; they, in fact, carried on the traditions of the Aurignacians; bone and ivory were used; and painting and drawing continued. Perhaps the most wonderful development of this time was the bone needle; at the beginning the sewing had been done in the same way that a shoemaker sews the sole of a shoe now, by boring a hole with a bone awl, and then passing a thread through. Of course, the Aurignacians had not any thread, but must have used fine sinews in this way. The next step was to hook the end of the awl so that the sinew could be pulled through, using the awl first to pierce the hole, and then as a crochet-needle to pull the thread through. The final step was to combine the two operations into one by the use of the needle, which pierced the hole, and carried the thread through itself (see A, B, and C, Fig. 52). To realize the joy of a Solutrean woman who first used a needle, let us imagine ourselves sewing to-day like a shoemaker, punching holes one at a time.

Fig. 52 shows a Solutrean needlemaker at work; first she cut a splinter of bone out of reindeer horn, as at 1. This was done by cutting a groove on each side with a flint graving tool, as at 2. The splinter was then shaved down with a scraper, as 3, and polished with a piece of stone, as 4, and the eye bored with a flint borer, as 5. You can see at the British Museum, the actual needles and the implements with which they were made, and it is worth a visit to see these. A sewing machine is a mechanically operated needle. At the British Museum you can see the start of the whole long business which led up to the sewing machine. Magdalenian women later on used hollow bones as needle-cases.

Though the Fourth Glacial period was now long past and the weather was gradually becoming more temperate, it did not improve in a regular way. The weather was colder than in Aurignacian times, and the mammoth and reindeer were still found in Europe.

MAGDALENIAN MAN

We can now pass on to the Magdalenian men, who succeeded the Solutreans. The typical station of the industry is on the Vézère, not far from the Castle of La Madeleine, hence the name. The Solutrean excelled in flint flaking, and the tool and the implement he made of it were both in this material. The Magdalenian used flint for his scrapers, borers, and gravers and finished them roughly. For the implements he made, he preferred bone and ivory. This detail at first may not seem of much importance, in reality it is as vital as if to-day we gave up steel and concrete and

153

started using some new material. Flint was to have a wonderful renaissance in Neolithic times, later on, before it slowly gave way to bronze. In many ways the Magdalenians appear to have been the descendants of the Aurignacians.

Magdalenian man appears to have been widely distributed over Europe. At Altamira, in Spain, he added the masterpieces of painting to the earlier drawings of the Aurignacians. He lived in France, Germany, and Belgium, and in England his handiwork has been found at Kent's Hole in Devon, and Cresswell Crags in Derbyshire. We are so anchored nowadays, with our houses to live in, and farms to raise foodstuffs, that it is difficult to realize this widespread distribution of prehistoric man, but in reality he needed far larger areas of land on which to hunt and find food. Prof. Sollas has an extremely interesting chapter in his book *Ancient Hunters*, in which he sums up the evidence of what Magdalenian man was like. So far as can be judged there were two types, the tall Crô-Magnons, and a shorter race like the Eskimos of to-day. A skeleton of the former was found again in the Vézère at Laugerie-Basse, Dordogne, in France, which had been buried in a contracted

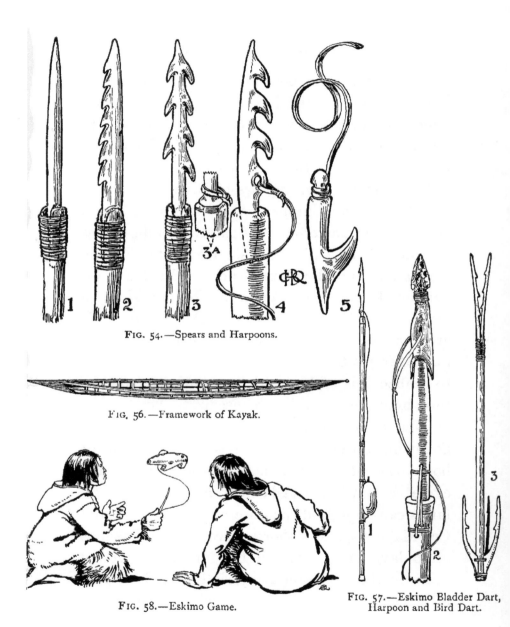

FIG. 54.—Spears and Harpoons.

FIG. 56.—Framework of Kayak.

FIG. 58.—Eskimo Game.

FIG. 57.—Eskimo Bladder Dart,
Harpoon and Bird Dart.

position with knees drawn up. Cowrie shells were found with the bones, and it is thought must have been sewn on to the clothing of the body, which was probably fully clothed when buried.

In 1888, another skeleton was found on the banks of the Beauronne, near Perigueux, Chancelade. It was of a shorter man than the Crô-Magnon, in many ways like the Combe Capelle type, the skull large and like those of the Eskimos to-day, with a ridge along the top. The head dolichocephalic and extraordinarily high. Fig. 53 gives some idea of the appearance of the Chancelade man. It has been suggested that he was the ancestor of the Eskimo, and was gradually pushed out of the fertile regions by the new race of men who came in Neolithic times, later on.

The climate was improving, and the Ice Age receding as a distant memory. The reindeer and mammoth were going north, and the Chancelade men, as hunters perhaps, followed their tracks, and so left the way open for the herdsmen and farmers who were to follow.

Magdalenian man made his spear and arrowheads in ivory and reindeer horn; these were spliced on to wooden shafts and consisted of long

157

lance-like points (as 1, Fig. 54). From these developed harpoons, first with one row of barbs, and then with two, as 2 and 3. This was a most useful discovery, that the barb would hold a fish after it had been speared; one can imagine the disgust of the early fisherman who lost his catch off the plain lance; his joy when he held it on the barbed harpoon. The first good fisherman's tale must have started with some such exploit. Spearing fish sounds a little unreal to-day, but there is an interesting account in Sir Walter Scott's *Redgauntlet*, of sport carried on in this way on horseback. "They chased the fish at full gallop, and struck them with their barbed spears." The scene is laid in the estuary of the Solway at low water, when the "waters had receded from the large and level space of sand, through which a stream, now feeble and fordable, found its way to the ocean." Magdalenian man must have had many a good day's sport like this. Out of the barb of the harpoon, the fish-hook must have developed. All this was possible in bone, though an impossibility in flint. Bone lends itself to decoration, and so the Magdalenian incised simple designs on his lance-heads. Smaller bone points have been

Fig. 55.—The Kayak.

found which suggest arrow-heads, but no bows. These being wooden would have decayed. This influence of material on design is very important; it is a very false and bad art which wastes material or tortures it into a shape which is unsuitable, so these early Magdalenians were proper designers, in that they used their material in a right way. The harpoons show them to have been fishermen and there are Magdalenian drawings of seal and salmon engraved on stone. One expects that the rivers then would have been like those in Western Canada to-day, where the salmon come up from the sea in tremendous quantities.

Nos. 3A and 4 (Fig. 54) show another interesting development of the harpoon. Magdalenian specimens have been found with a movable head, and this suggests that they were used in the same way as the harpoons of the Eskimos. No. 5 is our suggestion of how the fish-hook developed out of the barb of the harpoon. As there are many other points of resemblance between the Eskimo and the Magdalenians, we will see if any useful comparisons can be drawn.

The Eskimos are very widely distributed, as they must be, because they live by hunting. They depend on the seal, whale, and walrus for food and clothing, and these they hunt all along the Arctic coasts from Greenland to Alaska. They are a very gifted pleasant people, who have not any idea of war, because their main concern is a struggle for existence amidst ice and snow. They do not work iron, though in later days they have made use of any pieces which they could get hold of from traders. The Eskimo works in bone and wood in a really wonderful way, as we shall see. He also appears to have inherited the skill of the Magdalenian in drawing. Dr. Nansen writes of an Eskimo from Cape York, who "took a pencil, a thing he had never seen before, and sketched the coastline along Smith's Sound from his birthplace northwards with astonishing accuracy."

We will start with their methods of hunting. Seals are speared at blow-holes in the ice, but far more interesting are the methods by which they are harpooned in the open summer seas. The Eskimo then uses his kayak; this is a boat as Fig. 55, which varies somewhat in the various districts, but in all is constructed on the same principle. On the west coast of Greenland it is about seventeen feet long, and made of driftwood on a frame as Fig.

56, which is all bound together with thongs, and covered with sealskin. The kayak is decked over, and paddled with a double-bladed paddle. If we assume that the early Magdalenians were as clever as the Australians, and first made a bark canoe as Fig. 39, they would have found, as they left the rivers and ventured to sea, that the deck was an improvement. The harpoon with movable 'ead (as 4, Fig. 54) suggests that they did go to sea and attacked some larger quarry than the salmon. If they harpooned the seal with No. 3, the first convulsive plunge would have snapped off the head, and this was a precious possession. The head was made then to fit into a bone holder on the end of the lance, so that when the seal dived he wrenched it out of the holder only to find that it was still attached to the shaft by a leather thong. The Eskimo uses two harpoons, which are very beautiful developments of this idea.

No. 1, Fig. 57, shows their bladder dart. The head is removable and attached by a thong to the centre of the shaft, where in addition they fix a blown-up bladder. When the seal dives he is encumbered by the shaft, which is at right angles to the thong, and the bladder, which

163

also marks his position when he comes to the surface.

No. 2 shows the Eskimo harpoon. This had in old days an ivory head, tipped with flint, fitted on to a bone shaft. This latter is protected from snapping, by being attached to the wooden shaft with thongs in a sort of ball and socket joint. The line is attached to the ivory head, and then passes over a stud on the harpoon shaft; the loose line is carried on a holder on the kayak in front of the Eskimo, and the end is attached to a large sealskin float which rests at his back. The harpoon is thrown with a thrower in the same way that the Australian hurls his spears (Figs. 34 and 35). The head of the harpoon buries itself in the seal, and is so attached to the line that it turns at right angles in the wound. It is at once wrenched off the bone shaft, and the position of the seal is noted by the float which is thrown overboard. The wooden shaft floats and is picked up.

As there are many very beautiful ivory or bone harpoon-throwers of Magdalenian times, it seems fair to assume that the seal was hunted then as it is by the Eskimos to-day.

No. 3, Fig. 57, shows the bird-dart which is

thrown with a thrower. The forward projecting barbs kill the bird if the actual point misses. All these weapons are carried by the Eskimos on the deck of the kayak, neatly fitted under thongs and ivory studs.

The Eskimo's clothing is of sealskin, and his coat is arranged to fit closely around the circular rim of the hole in the deck in which he sits. He can be tumbled right over by a rough sea, and yet right himself with a turn of the paddle.

The Magdalenian had bone needles, and his clothing may have been like this.

At the British Museum there is a sledge made of driftwood, with bone platings on the runners, all tied up with thongs. It should be seen to realize how primitive man manages without nails and screws. As well there are kayaks and a model of the umiak or women's boat. Fig. 58 shows an Eskimo game played rather like cup and ball. A very much simplified Polar bear is carved in ivory and pierced with many holes; the bear has to be caught through one of the holes on the end of the stick.

The boring of holes brings up the question of whether Magdalenian man used the bow-drill.

Everyday Life in the Old Stone Age

Small ivory rods have been found, perforated at one end, with a slit at the other shaped into a mouth. This is thought to have been the bow. The bowstring was tied through the hole at one end, given a twist round the drill, and the bow then being bent, a loop in the bowstring was slipped into the notched end of the bow, and kept the latter bent. Our cut (Fig. 47) shows how the drill could then be rotated. Such drills are used by the Eskimos, and many other primitive people to-day, both to bore holes and produce fire by friction.

Drawings have been discovered which are thought to represent tents or huts, and suggest that the Magdalenians had improved on those of the Aurignacians, as shown in Fig. 44. This round bee-hive form, made perhaps of willow withies, would have been weak in the crown, if the tent was of any size, yet it could be constructed very simply anywhere that saplings were found. One of the Magdalenian drawings suggests a type, as Fig. 59. Almost all the early hut builders seem to have dug a hole in the ground of circular shape. The earth removed was heaped up round the outside. In the centre of the hole a roof tree was set up, formed

FIG. 59.—Type of Huts suggested by Magdalenian drawings

FIG. 60.—Type of Huts suggested by Magdalenian drawings.

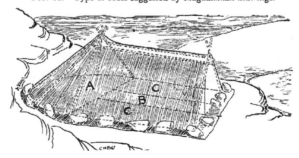

FIG. 61.—Eskimo Summer Tent.

of the trunk of a tree, with a fork perhaps left at the top. Around this saplings were placed, their feet stuck into the surrounding mound, with the tops leaning against the roof tree. These formed the rafters, and if in between these were interlaced smaller boughs, it is quite easy to see that the whole could be covered with skins or rough grass thatch. Quite a comfortable little house could be made in this way, and we know that it is a type which was general in Neolithic times.

Other Magdalenian drawings suggest a type, as Fig. 60, and this is a form of hut which is constructed by the North American Indians.

The Magdalenians had their winter quarters in caves and rock shelters and the period is named after the cave of La Madeleine on the banks of the Vézère. Did Magdalenian man, as he slowly travelled to the north, take with him a memory of the rock shelters of France, and hand down a building tradition to the Eskimos of to-day? They have very interesting rock houses, and others which are constructed in a skilful way with blocks of snow. Stone lamps have been discovered, which suggest that the Magdalenian not only lighted but warmed his houses, as the Eskimo does to-day, by burning fat in a stone lamp with a moss wick.

Fig. 61 shows the skin tent which the Eskimo uses on his summer wanderings. The plan resembles that of the houses; there is the semicircular bed-place at A, and a central gangway at B, with cooking pots at the sides at C. The diagram shows how the tent is made with poles and covered with skins, the front portion being of membrane to admit light. Large stones serve to hold down the skins. We have included these drawings because we want to get as many representative types as we can of primitive dwelling-places. We shall find it useful later on.

The Magdalenian, like the Eskimo, may have used his lamp for cooking, but here is an interesting description by Darwin of a Tahitian who prepared a meal in another way: "Having made a small fire of sticks, placed a score of stones, of about the size of cricket balls, on the burning wood. In about ten minutes, the sticks were consumed, and the stones hot. They had previously folded up in small parcels of leaves, pieces of beef, fish, ripe and unripe bananas, and the tops of the wild arum. These green parcels were laid in a layer between

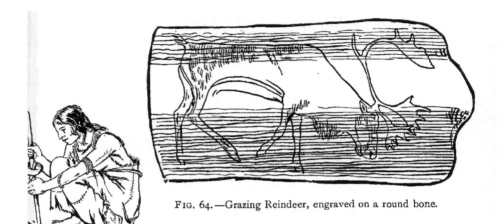

FIG. 64.—Grazing Reindeer, engraved on a round bone.

G. 62.—Digging-stick.

FIG. 65.—Deer crossing a Stream, engraved on a round bone.

two layers of the hot stones, and the whole then covered up with earth, so that no smoke or steam could escape. In about a quarter of an hour, the whole was most deliciously cooked." This was a method used in Neolithic times later on. The Magdalenians may have used the reindeer for food in the winter, by drying the flesh over a wood fire, and then pounding it up, and preserving it by pouring over hot fat, rather like the pemmican of the Indian and Eskimo.

We cannot be sure whether the Magdalenians had started cultivating the soil. Perforated stones have been found which may have been used to load the digging-stick, as Fig. 62. This is the method the Bushmen adopt, and Darwin mentioned the use of the digging-stick in Chile, to dig up roots, though this does not mean cultivating them.

The Magdalenian period marked the highest development of the art of prehistoric man. The paintings are of astonishing merit; without being great sticklers for detail, these old painters caught the very spirit of the animals they painted. The mammoth swings along alive from the tip of his trunk to the end of his tufted tail. The bison and boar charge; the reindeer and red deer move in a slow, easy canter. The drawings are proof of the immensely developed power of detailed observation which came to the hunter as part of his craft, and which is different to the sympathy shown in later days, when animals were domesticated. Fig. 63 shows a Magdalenian painting of a boar, and the frontispiece, Fig. 1, a bison, from the Altamira Cave.

The artists of those days used reds and browns, blacks and yellows, and were adepts at producing high lights, half-tones, and shadow. They appear to have started with a black outline, and then to have fitted in the body of the work, adding tone, or wiping away colour to get the effect of lights. The figures are often of life size, and their vigour makes us wish that we could draw animals in such a living way.

M. Daleau has found in France, red oxide of iron, which formed the basis of one of the colours, the pestles with which it was ground, and the shoulder blades of animals that served as palettes. Brushes were used, and would not have been difficult to make. The paints were carried in little tubes made of reindeer horn; truly there is nothing new under the sun, and we shall find some day, per-

Fig. 63.—Magdalenian Cave Painting.

haps, a catalogue of a Magdalenian artists' colour-man. We have said that these old painters caught the very spirit of the animals they drew, and to do this they realized that it was necessary to compose, or design, their shapes and outlines. To-day we can snapshot a horse while galloping, and the resulting photograph will not convey the sense of action that the Palæolithic artist has obtained in Fig. 63. This is because the human eye cannot record movement with the rapidity of the lens of a camera. The artist realizes this, and presents instead a convention, or design, which we find more real than the reality of the photograph.

The Magdalenian engravings on ivory, sometimes on the handles of their shaft-straighteners, were just as wonderful as the paintings. There is one in the British Museum from La Madeleine, of a mammoth which is splendid in its vigour. Figs. 64 and 65 are fine examples of engraving on bone. Fig. 66, of an ivory dagger at the British Museum, shows that Magdalenian man could carve in the round, as well as cut an incised line. Fig. 67 shows a harpoon-thrower, the use of which was described. Remember that all the engraving and carving was done with flint implements.

The drawings and engravings convince us that the artists knew the animals, and that their work was actual life-drawing; in this way we can find that among the Magdalenian animals were mammoth, reindeer, and the great Irish deer, the bison and horse, the musk ox, glutton, and Arctic hare. These show that the climate was for some part of the Magdalenian period colder than in Aurignacian times.

The illustrations we have given are sufficient to prove that the Magdalenians were a very highly gifted race. These people were becoming civilized, and they were artists, and so would have been pleasant and friendly. We cannot say how they said "How do you do" to one another; perhaps like the New Zealanders they rubbed noses. Darwin when he went there wrote: "They then squatted themselves down and held up their faces; my companion standing over them, one after another, placed the bridge of his nose at right angles to theirs, and commenced pressing. This lasted rather longer than a cordial shake of the hand with us; and as we vary the force of the grasp of the hand in shaking so they do in pressing. During the process they uttered comfortable little grunts."

Artists of the Old Stone Age

To sum up, if it is correct that certain bone rods which have been found at Aurignacian stations in France are the bows of bow-drills, as Fig. 47, then this must be noted as another very considerable step forward. It is obvious that the Aurignacians must have had some ready method for drilling their shaft-straighteners as Fig. 46. The bow-drill led to the modern lathe. We shall see that in later times the people knew how to turn quite well, and it is probable that they used a type of the primitive pole lathe. In this the rotary movement was conveyed, to the article to be turned, by a rope which was passed around it in the same way that the bowstring was applied to the drill to turn it. The potter's wheel, which again follows later on, is descended from the bow-drill.

At the end of the third chapter we suggested that man, at first only concerned with food, had begun to realize that there was a spiritual side to his nature. In Magdalenian times we find the manifestations of this in an appreciation of beauty; there were artists in those days.

Now Art is a much maligned word; it really means *doing* things, whereas science is *knowing* things. People nowadays think of an artist as a painter; we should like to define that individual as any man, or woman, who puts more into a job of work than they expect to take out of it; the business man is one who wants to take out a little more than he puts in.

We should like to point out that an engineer may be a very good artist. A fine motor-car is a work of Art; it has Beauty of form, and is designed with Truth, or it would not do its job, so that it possesses two of the great qualities; there remains only Goodness. It therefore follows that no man can do fine work unless he has some appreciation of the underlying principles on which humanity has built itself up. At the very worst he can only be one third bad, so credit must be given to the artists of all kinds.

We like to think that good work has been one of the prime factors in the civilization of man, and we believe that dull mechanical work destroys the brain. If this is so, what of the poor factory hand of to-day, chained to the machine as its slave? It is not possible for him to dream dreams, or see visions; the utmost limit of his, or her, endeavour, is, perhaps, to watch an automatic machine making nuts, each an exact counterpart of its fellow.

Artists of the Old Stone Age

We wonder, when our turn comes to be dug up and have our skulls measured, say in 5000 A.D., if the archæologists of that far-away to-morrow will say, Here was a people who threw away their heritage, and arrested their development, because they lost the use of their hands.

But so far as our friends the Magdalenians are concerned, judged by their work they had made great advances, and, like the Eskimos whom they so closely resembled, must have been a pleasant people.

CHAPTER V

THE Azilians, who followed after the Magdalenians, were the last people of the Old Stone Age. After this we come to Neolithic times, or the New Stone Age. The Azilians, like all these early peoples, were widely distributed, and traces of their handiwork have been found as far apart as the cave of Mas d'Azil, Ariège, near Lourdes in the south of France, and Sevenoaks and Hastings in England, and Oban in Scotland. The Scottish discoveries of harpoons are very interesting. It shows that the ice was retreating, and man making his way into the tracts of the newly uncovered land.

We know what some of the Azilians were like because they had a curious habit of removing the heads from the bodies of their dead and burying the skulls like eggs in nests. At the Ofnet Cave, near Nördlingen, Bavaria, South Germany, twenty-seven were found together buried in red ochre. This would suggest that the Azilians used to

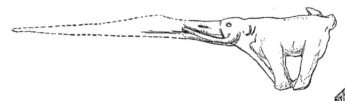

FIG. 66.—Magdalenian Carved Ivory Dagger.

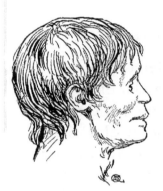

FIG. 68.—Round-headed
Ofnet Man.

FIG. 69.—Long-headed
Ofnet Man.

FIG. 70.—Azilian
Painted Stones.

FIG. 67.—Magdalen-
ian Carved Ivory
Harpoon-thrower.

The End of the Old Stone Age

paint their bodies in their lifetime, and so the colour was buried with them for use in the spirit world. One skull of a small child had many shells placed near it—perhaps as play-things. Round another was a chaplet of deer's teeth, and all were placed in the same way, looking westward. The actual bodies were probably consumed by fire; later on cremation was a usual method, the ashes being buried in an urn.

Here is a new fact; most of the old races we have been writing about were long-headed (dolicho-cephalic); we now find side by side with this type, brachycephalic, or a rounder-headed people. The fact that individuals of the two races were buried in the same grave points to their having lived to-gether happily. So that if some Magdalenians moved north after the mammoth and the reindeer, others remained behind.

Our drawing (Fig. 68) has been made from the rounder-headed Ofnet skull. Fig. 69 is of the longer-headed type.

We do not find any beautiful paintings in this period. Man was beginning to look on animals from a different point of view. In the old days he had the hunter's eye, quick to note beauty of body and grace of movement, which he expressed in drawings; in Azilian days he may have begun to look on himself as a herdsman, though so far only the dog was domesticated. The climate was milder, with westerly winds and warm rains; the waters were rising. Great Britain was an island, and great forests spread over the land, except where the Loess lay thick, and by fineness prevented the trees from taking root. Man, who had been free to roam over the tundra, was now hemmed in, so the old care-free life passed away, and he began to have possessions.

These had to be useful, and we do not find any cunning work in ivory. The awl takes the place of the needle. Flint is revived for making implements, but in a rougher way than those of Solutrean times. Stag horn is used for harpoons instead of reindeer, so the Azilians also were fishermen.

The most interesting things which they have left behind them are the painted stones found at Mas d'Azil. These are flattish in shape, about two inches across, and painted with signs, as Fig. 70. Some of them are surprisingly like early forms of letters—red and black were used. The use to which these stones were put is unknown, but they

The End of the Old Stone Age

may have been tallies or accounts. If to-day you ask a labouring man to cart bricks or tiles, and keep count, he will do so in tens. These he chalks up on the barn door, and obtains his hundreds by ten tens. So these stones may have been tokens or tallies used by Azilian man in keeping the accounts of his trade by barter. We can be quite sure that some sort of trade had been in existence even long before this time. We have seen on p. 155 how cowrie shells were found with the Crô-Magnon type of skeleton at Laugerie-Basse. Four were near the head, and two at each elbow, knee, and foot. They must have been sewn on the clothing. These would have come from the Mediterranean, and would have been rarities in the centre of France. The chiefs would have desired them on the principle that fine feathers, or shells, make fine birds, or men. So perhaps skins or harpoons were given in exchange. Don't be amused at these simple folk, because the exchange of commodities still remains as the basis of our trade, and we use money or bills of exchange as tallies or tokens. Life was becoming easier, and was perhaps not so much of a desperate struggle for survival as it had been.

Everyday Life in the Old Stone Age

The Glacial Period had receded into the past, and the climate was temperate. Whereas in Magdalenian times the countryside had the appearance of the Arctic tundra where the Eskimos now live, in Azilian times it became well wooded.

Before we leave the painted stones, we must draw attention to the fact that some of the markings are very much like Roman letters. From this some archæologists have argued that the stones were the text-books from which Azilian boys learned their A B C. This is a tremendous flight of imagination, and a short cut indeed at the same time. We feel that the Roman letter had to wait for thousands of years yet before it arrived at the character we know now. Turn the subject over in your mind, and think how prehistoric man conveyed information or asked for it. Our early friend, the Java sub-man, had rudimentary powers of speech; he progressed as a baby does now. Our own very youngest brother learns to say "bread," because his small brain teaches him that this is what the grown-ups call the stuff which is so pleasant to eat; speech comes first, then letters. All letters seem to have started as pictures. We know pre-

The End of the Old Stone Age

historic man could draw splendidly; if he met a man who did not understand his own language, he would naturally draw the thing he desired to obtain. We remember once buying a goose in Wales, from an old lady who spoke only Welsh, which we did not understand. We pointed to the goose, and by signs conveyed the idea that we wished to buy it. We then in the same way invited her to take as much money from our hand as she desired; but we wished her to kill, draw, and deliver the bird in time for dinner the next day, at a farm some miles away. So to the great delight of the old lady we drew pictures of the doom and journeyings of the goose, and in due course we dined off it; but this would be a very laborious method for all the actions of everyday life. The drawings then were standardized and simplified and in time became letters, and our old A B C, like everything else, has behind it a history stretching out across the horizons into the very beginnings of time itself. Our readers will know Kipling's delightful tale of *How the Alphabet was made*, in "Just So Stories."

The probable Azilian deposits at Oban were found in a cave opening on to a sea-beach. Prof.

Everyday Life in the Old Stone Age

Sollas mentions the fact that in a beach at Glasgow, which corresponds in age with the one at Oban, no less than eighteen dug-out canoes have been discovered. These may have belonged to Azilian man. On the rocky floor of the cave at Oban were successive deposits: first a pebbly gravel washed in by high tides, then a bed of shells, then gravel, and on top of this another shell-bed with a final topping of black earth, formed in later ages. The level of the land has gone up, perhaps as it lost its tremendous load of ice, or that of the sea gone down, because the cave is now some thirty feet above the sea-level.

In the shell-beds are shells of oysters, limpets, whelks, the claws of lobsters, the bones of large sea fish, red deer, goat, pig, and many other animals. Ashes remain where the cooking hearths were. From all these remains we can be quite sure that Azilian man was both fisherman and hunter, and the bones of the large sea fish mean that he took his harpoon to sea, in some form of canoe, or boat, covered with skins.

Man about this time seems to have been drawn more and more to the water. In Norway and Sweden, Azilian remains have been found which

The End of the Old Stone Age

point to dwellings built on enormous rafts anchored in lakes. All sorts of implements fell through the logs of which the rafts were composed, and have since been discovered in the peat which has formed in the old lake beds. Flint implements were used, and harpoons, spear-heads, and fish-hooks. The bones of dogs have been found, and it is thought this proves that they were domesticated by the Azilians.

We do not know why man should have chosen such strange homes for himself and his family; probably fear drove him there, but he had now no foes to fear like the sabre-toothed tiger. That fierce animal had long since gone; perhaps it was the most terrible foe of all, his fellow-man, of equal cunning with himself, and far more subtle than the clumsy mammoth, that compelled him to take refuge on the water. We shall see how in Neolithic times he built the Lake Dwellings on piles, and lived over the water, as he does to-day in New Guinea. If at about this time the dog became the friend of man, then again this marks another very notable step, and it would be extremely interesting to know how the long friendship began. Kipling in the "Just So Stories" gives us an idea. It

Everyday Life in the Old Stone Age

is a proof of great intelligence on the part of prehistoric man, because the dog would have been as useful an ally as fire and flint, as well as being an excellent companion. It is almost impossible for us to imagine a world to-day with only wild dogs and wolves in it.

We wanted to sum up the general impressions to be gathered from the life of prehistoric man, and the dog gives us the opportunity of doing so, by showing the difference that he made to man when they became friends.

We have seen that the most urgent need of prehistoric man was food; that as he had not domesticated any of the animals, except the dog, and did not grow any corn, he had to hunt to live, and was a wanderer because he followed the game. When the dog came as a friend, he brought an even keener sense of smell than that of prehistoric man, and so could follow the trail; at the same time he would have simplified the task of stalking the animals. It was necessary to get within the limited range of a spear thrown by hand, before prehistoric man could kill his supper, and the dog would have helped by driving the game towards the hunter.

The End of the Old Stone Age

With a more acute sense of hearing, the dog would have given prehistoric man the feeling of security which he so badly needed. The man would have been afraid of so many things; the nasty little noises of the night would have alarmed him so much more than the howling of wolves which he knew; there was the constant dread of magic and evil spirits. Prehistoric man then, crouching at the side of his camp-fire, looked out into encircling gloom and saw the firelight reflected in the eyes of wild animals with more assurance when he had the dog beside him for a friend; if the supper had to be shared, the dangers seemed to be halved.

If we go back and think of the other things we have written about, we must bear in mind that the ancient hunters were helped in their wanderings by a differently shaped Europe to the one we know today. The isthmuses at Sicily, Gibraltar, and Dover, not only led to wide wanderings on the part of Palæolithic man, but opened the way for interesting migration of animals. The Southern types could come North, and the Northern go South if need be.

Great climatic changes, like the Ice Ages, played their part in man's development, by adding the stern necessity of altering his mode of life, if he wished to survive. We look back on a Europe of those days, as on a broad but dimly lighted stage. Across it pass the huge *E. antiquus*, the hippo, and sabre-toothed tiger, later come the mammoth and reindeer, with hyænas, lions, and bears; and man moves among them and seems to have changed least of any.

Mr. Crawford, in his book *Man and his Past*, has taken an idea from Samuel Butler's *Life and Habit*, and applied it to prehistoric man; it amounts to this, that man by the use of tools has added limbs to himself. He rides a bicycle to-day and, by the use of gears, progresses as rapidly as if he had as many legs as a centipede. A flint implement was as useful to prehistoric man as another hand.

No animal uses tools; they will use beak, claw, and tail as tools, which is a different matter. Man then, in times of great changes, was not called upon to alter his own body, to suit the altered circumstances. The animal does this, or rather in many generations, and at the cost of countless lives, it is done, or, as in the case of the great reptiles, the type becomes extinct. The weather becoming colder, the animal will gradually de-

The End of the Old Stone Age

velop and grow a thicker coat, but man, with his tool, makes himself one quickly, and so leaves time to do all sorts of other things as well.

In using his tools, man was worried and made to think; his brain and soul, chained up in the clumsy body, were stimulated by this endeavour to do work. It is this tool-using habit of man, and all that it means, which makes the early flint implements so interesting; the hand-axes and scrapers, the borers and burins, have been prime factors in civilization, and their utility has many times meant the difference between life and death to whole races.

Then we have the tremendous revelation of Magdalenian art, blazing up in the middle of the Stone Age, and then the flame being extinguished; how did this come about? In any summary of the Old Stone Age, there is always this problem to be thought of.

It was the tools of prehistoric man which made possible the beginnings of so many other things. The harpoon must have been used from some sort of boat or canoe. The huts have developed into our houses; the perforated wolf's fangs, or cowrie shells, strung together as a necklet, and the hollow base of a mammoth's tusk sawn off as a bracelet, led the way for all the other people who wanted to make themselves beautiful. Bone needles made fine sewing and embroidery possible; all this is part and parcel of archæology, and there still remains plenty to do.

Archæology is like the design of a Roman pavement, built up of many small fragments, or tesseræ. The main design is beginning to be known, but many of the details are missing. It is for this reason that research work goes on; that camps are dug over, and ancient cities uncovered. Many months' work may result in just one small piece of new knowledge. The archæologist is delighted, and tells all his friends, and the little new tessera is fitted into its place in the larger pattern; but first it is tested in all ways, to see that it really fits, because these people are learned, and jealous that before any addition is made it shall be real knowledge.

If this book has given any of our readers any idea of even the outline of the pattern of this knowledge, we shall be very happy, because they can then start serious work on their own account. We can then pass on to how Neolithic man carried on

The End of the Old Stone Age

his everyday life, which will be the subject of our next book. And now, in the friendliest way possible, we should like to take leave of our readers for a little time.

"The Dance" by P. C. Q.

INDEX

Index

Index

Edited by Prof. J. ARTHUR THOMSON

*4 vols. Royal Octavo. Nearly 1000 Illustrations
Including 40 Large Plates in Color*

The wonderful story of effort, of advancement, of accomplishment, and of the evolution of the sciences of today from the earlier conceptions and theories of our ancestors, told in plain language, free from technical terms.

Here is the story of the progress of Science, of results obtained, conclusions drawn, and facts verified, by the most eminent students in all branches of science. These writers have sought to open up their various subjects, as one might on a walk with a friend, and have succeeded so admirably that the work might be termed Informal Introductions to the Various Departments of Knowledge.

The Editor needs no introduction to Scientific Circles, and no writer of today is capable of a greater gift of luminous expression—always vividly alive, illustrative, and suggestive.

In *The Outline of Science*, the advance and amazing developments of modern science are set clearly and in simply expressed language before the vast non-scientific public.

New York   **G. P. Putnam's Sons**   London

The
A B C of Evolution

By
Joseph McCabe

A book that tells the meaning of Evolution, and the actual story of the evolution of things, in very simple and attractive language. Packed with scientific knowledge, but quite free from difficult scientific terms. Tells you about everything, from Einstein to the Brontosaur, from the stars to the laws of social development, yet a child may read it with pleasure.

G. P. Putnam's Sons

New York   London

Ingram Content Group UK Ltd.
Milton Keynes UK
UKHW020054100623
423210UK00005B/112